THE REALLY USEFUL
GUIDE TO WHITE WINE

SUSY
ATKINS

THE REALLY USEFUL GUIDE TO WHITE WINE.

EDITORIAL DIRECTOR Jane O'Shea
CREATIVE DIRECTOR Helen Lewis
PROJECT EDITOR Lisa Pendreigh
EDITOR Laura Herring
DESIGNER Claire Peters
PHOTOGRAPHER William Reavell
PRODUCTION Funsho Asemota

First published in 2006 by
Quadrille Publishing Ltd
Alhambra House
27–31 Charing Cross Road
London WC2H 0LS

Reprinted in 2006
10 9 8 7 6 5 4 3 2

Text © 2003, 2006 Susy Atkins
Design and layout © 2006
Quadrille Publishing Ltd

Originally published exclusively
for J Sainsbury plc.

The right of Susy Atkins to be identified
as Author of this Work has been asserted
by her in accordance with the Copyright,
Designs and Patents Act 1988.

Cataloguing in Publication Data: a catalogue
record for this book is available from the
British Library.

ISBN-13: 978 184400 291 7
ISBN-10: 1 84400 291 8
Printed in China

CONTENTS

SO MANY PEOPLE ARE NOW FASCINATED BY WINE. It is cherished by adults from all walks of life – male and female, young and old. We adore not only expensive bottles of Champagne and Chablis, but everyday bottles from all corners of the world, too. This is partly because the quality has improved greatly over the past twenty years. Then there is the increased availability of good wines so that we are all within easy reach of exciting and unusual flavours.

Yet wine is still seen by some as mystifying, even intimidating. What a shame! True, it is a complicated subject to grasp – today there are so many styles of wine, grapes and regions, that trying to find out more can be daunting. And perhaps that is especially true of white wines. It is so much easier to buy yet another bottle of Aussie Chardonnay or Italian Pinot Grigio, or to stick to a reliable (if bland) big brand name.

But how boring that is! This book makes learning about wine an enjoyable and easy experience. Here are the essential white wine styles: from the light, dry whites; fruity, spicy whites to rich, oaky whites and sparklers. Get tasting the wines you find here: it is the only way to pin down your own likes and dislikes. There are hints on great food matches, and tips on how to buy, store and serve the various white wines, too, so you can get the most out of them.

You'll notice a few recommended labels or wineries throughout the book. These are names I rate, but be aware it is nowhere near a comprehensive list and indeed in some larger regions I have sometimes avoided specific recommendations – there simply wasn't room. In short, where there are recommendations, these make good starting points, but there are plenty more great wines to discover!

THEIR DETRACTORS WRITE OFF THE LIGHT, DRY WHITES AS BORING AND FLAVOURLESS, BUT THOSE IN THE KNOW POINT TO SOME OF THESE WINES AS THE MOST ELEGANT AND REFRESHING AROUND. A few are even complex and satisfying, although you will unfortunately encounter some flavourless, mediocre bottles along the way. A premium light, dry white has a lovely crispness, subtle fruit flavours and, perhaps, a pretty, aromatic hint of blossom. It may be delicate, but a good light white wakes up the palate, makes the mouth water and whets the appetite like no other table wine. It also washes down a range of summery dishes wonderfully well – leafy salads, white fish and pasta in creamy sauces. And the greatest quality is how easygoing and enjoyable it is – unlike, say, a heavily oaked Chardonnay that may effortlessly win a wine competition, but which you don't want to drink in any great quantity. Light, dry whites should always be highly drinkable and moreish.

So, how can you avoid those dull bottles? Cool climates count for a lot; pick a wine from a place where the grapes retain pure fruit flavours and that essential 'zing' of acidity. Warm climates just don't do the same trick. Go for the better grape varieties – Riesling, Verdicchio and Grüner Veltliner – which are more likely to make wine with flavour, rather than second-rate ones – Müller-Thurgau and Trebbiano – which tend to produce uninspiring, bland whites. Riesling, in particular, is in a league of its own. With all light, dry whites, try to track down a winemaker who uses low-yielding vines (for more concentration in the grapes) rather than fertile, high-cropping ones. Not much on the label will tell you this, but some of the tips on the next few pages will point you towards the right wines. Trading up a notch from the basic, rustic whites, churned out as cheap-and-cheerful gluggers, will help you avoid the sort of wine that's a yawn and instead give you a crisp, zesty wake-up call to the senses!

APPEARANCE

Pale-straw colour, sometimes with light-green hints. Not golden-yellow like richer or sweeter white wines.

TEXTURE

Relatively thin, light, watery, neither viscous nor weighty.

AROMA

Good examples smell of fresh, tangy citrus fruit: lemons, limes, grapefruit, and crunchy green apples. Some have a floral note, others a hint of almond. Second-rate, dull examples have little aroma or smell grubby.

FLAVOUR

Should have a refreshing, succulent streak of acidity. Again, look out for those citrus fruits and freshly chopped apples. A clean, crisp, mineral finish.

RIESLING

NATURALLY LIGHT AND ELEGANT

The Riesling grape is refreshing in more ways than one. Of course, as anyone who has tried true Riesling will know, it is one of the world's greatest aperitifs – naturally light and elegant yet racy, with mouth-watering citrus and apple fruit and quite a crisp finish. So it's refreshing in the most obvious sense of the word. But Riesling is also refreshing in that it makes a welcome change from all the Chardonnay and Sauvignon Blanc that fills our shop shelves.

It is a quite different style of wine, as will become clear below. But why the need to say 'true' Riesling? That's because this poor grape gets blamed – unfairly – for much of the light, white dross out there. Many have the wrong idea about Riesling; they think it's the variety behind the blandest, least memorable light whites, when cheaper, less well-known grapes are usually responsible. If I handed you a glass of fine Riesling, you'd probably be amazed at how much delicious flavour there is – and how tangy, vivacious and delightfully fresh the wine seems. So, don't confuse Riesling with lesser wines. It's consistently delightful, and remarkably long-lived to boot. In fact, for many serious wine buffs, this is the greatest white grape of all.

GERMANY

Fine German Riesling is a very different creature from cheap and nasty German plonk, so if you've never tried it, give it a go. It's no surprise that this type of wine is often described as one of the trade's best kept secrets – plenty of aficionados out there love it despite its untrendy image! A cool climate produces wines that are never over-the-top – restraint, subtlety and elegance are the watchwords. Alcohol levels remain naturally low – seven or eight percent is not unusual, and nine or ten percent is quite common (compared to twelve to fourteen percent in many other table wines).

That said, the style does vary from bottle to bottle – too much so at times, as it can be hard to know exactly what type of Riesling you are getting by looking at the label. Here are some tips: the Mosel region makes the prettiest, most delicate examples, with a spring-like, apple-blossom scent, although there is still a spine-tingling acidity in many; the Rheingau makes more intense, fuller-bodied versions, while the Pfalz is a progressive region, turning out more juicy, fruity, modern styles.

The main problem is picking a level of sweetness you enjoy – whether it's bone-dry and bracing, medium with a dab of honeyed weight or luscious and sticky. Germany makes Riesling at all levels of sweetness, but the most densely written Gothic labels are not easy to read. Incidentally, this is one reason fine German wines have gone out of fashion – consumers find the words on, say, an Australian bottle much easier to follow.

For the record: the word *trocken* on a label means dry, while *halbtrocken* means semi-dry. Meanwhile, the top quality category of Riesling (these bottles say *Qualitätswein mit Prädikat* or QmP on the label), ones made according to certain strict rules and regulations, are divided into six categories according to the ripeness of the grapes used, and this (rather roughly) corresponds to their dryness/sweetness levels. *Kabinett* indicates dry, *Spätlese* is a riper, often off-dry style, and *Auslese*, *Beerenauslese*, *Trockenbeerenauslese* and *Eiswein* follow next in order of increasing sweetness. Then there are certain wines which have been made from fruit grown in the best sites – *Erstes Gewächs*, or 'first growth'. These specific vineyard areas are named on the label.

Complicated? Yes. German Riesling does takes a bit of getting to know. But it is worth it. Once you have convinced yourself, try these tantalising, lip-smacking whites on your friends; if they are dubious, then let them taste it before telling them it's a German wine. I bet most of them will love it and will be converted to the joys of Riesling.

On the other hand, there are some small signs now that German Riesling is set to become a bit more fashionable. Most people have got over their obsession with chunky, oaky southern hemisphere whites and recognise that there are other, more subtle, white wines out there. The prices are also fair – very fair, in fact – and a good Riesling is also wonderfully food-friendly in a way that a monster Californian Chardonnay will never be.

Finally, don't miss the chance to try an older German Riesling. If it is stored correctly, it will lose its spiky, acid edge, softening and mellowing, and taking on a more honeyed, toffee-apple appeal. Then there's

something else about older Riesling – it acquires a distinct whiff of lanolin and petrol. That sounds horrible, but it isn't; instead, it gives a lovely warm, mellow richness to the older wines. Give them a go – you have to try aged Riesling for yourself to see just what I mean. Once you've started drinking German Riesling, you can start to become an expert by comparing wines from particular vineyard sites, as they give a fascinating insight into the effects of different soils and micro-climates.

FRANCE

The second-best place in the world for producing Riesling is Alsace in eastern France. This region is on the French border with Germany and has at several times during its history been part of Germany, so it's hardly surprising that Riesling is an important grape here. Wines that come from Alsace can even look confusingly Germanic, with a tall bottle shape, Germanic names and sometimes Gothic script on the label, so be careful to distinguish the two – they are quite different in taste. Alsace Rieslings have a richer, more full-bodied character, and the alcohol levels are usually higher – back up to normal table-wine levels rather than unusually low. They should still have that tell-tale streak of fresh acidity, though, and the best examples should age well.

Look out for the prestigious *grand cru* wines – over fifty of the best vineyard sites (*grands crus*, named on the label) are meant to indicate the best fruit in the region. Some are superb, but others just don't quite deserve the honour and extra cost that a *grand cru* wine can fetch. Match them with richer food than the German Rieslings, such as a cheese-and-onion tart or fish in creamy sauces. Good producers are: Trimbach, Zind-Humbrecht and, for good value, Turckheim.

REST OF EUROPE

Austria makes some impressive dry Riesling, with tart, intense lemon fruit and a bracing mineral quality. Some have a weighty, full texture (expect thirteen percent alcohol – much higher than in Germany) and should age well. Try one made near to Vienna or from the region of Styria or, best of all, from the Wachau region in Lower Austria, where the cool climate and well-drained soils help create some brilliant wines. Bründlmayer, Hirtzberger, FX Pichler are names to look out for. A few rather lean, but refreshing Rieslings are made in northern Italy, mostly in the cool northeast of the country. Go for wines produced in the Trentino or Alto-Adige regions.

REST OF THE WORLD

Australian Riesling is a 'must-try' – you will see a completely different side to the grape. Sure, the crisp acidity is still there, and that citrus fruit is to the fore, but this is a riper type of Riesling, a sun-kissed wine, with juicy lime the most obvious characteristic. If it is given enough time (five years or more), that crisp edge softens and toasty, honeyed layers begin to appear, while that freshly chopped fruit becomes more like lime marmalade... Delicious! A suggestion of petrol or kerosene can also be identified in a properly matured example.

Clare Valley and Eden Valley (both in the south) and Tasmania are key regions for producing good quality Australian Riesling. Interestingly, before the boom in Chardonnay plantings, Riesling was the most widely planted white grape Down Under, and now winemakers seem to have revived their interest, so look out for a growing number appearing on the shelves. Good labels to try include: Mount Langi Ghiran, Tim Adams and Henschke, and at the cheaper end, even the Jacob's Creek Riesling is a corker!

While we're in the Antipodes, don't miss out on New Zealand Riesling. It's similar to the Australian style, bursting with citrus fruit, but has a pithier, more mineral-dry edge. The South Island wine regions make the best – especially Marlborough, Central Otago and Waipara/Canterbury. Felton Road, Giesen, Villa Maria and Hunter's all produce fine examples.

Canada is another country excelling with dry Riesling – it's a pity the wines are not more widely available. The sweet Rieslings of Canada are more renowned but if you come across a dry one, snap it up. In the United States, most wine is sourced from California, but not Riesling. Although a very few decent West Coast examples do exist (from high-altitude, cool sites), better Riesling has come out of Washington State, Oregon and the Finger Lakes in New York State, where winemakers concentrated on this variety while the Californians went mad for Chardonnay.

SAUVIGNON BLANC

LIGHT AND LEAN STYLES

Sauvignon Blanc can often be very fruity and pungent, and because of this the grape is dealt with in more detail in the next chapter, 'Fruity, Spicy Whites' (see pages 48–53). Nonetheless, light, lean Sauvignons do exist in the form of Sancerre and Pouilly-Fumé and other wines from the cool Loire Valley.

FRANCE

Sancerre is perhaps the most famous appellation for Sauvignon Blanc – it produces extremely attractive, bone-dry, lemony wines, while nearby Pouilly-Fumé wines are known for their mineral, slightly smoky note (think of a spark of gun-flint; the whiff of smoke from a fired pistol). The best vineyards where these wines are produced have chalk over clay soils, with some patches of flint, the latter known as silex soils and said to produce the most long-lived wines. Top Sancerre and Pouilly-Fumé are, for many, the most elegant and hauntingly beautiful Sauvignons of all, and from a fine winemaker such as Cotat Frères, De Ladoucette or Didier Dagueneau, so they are, but many inferior wines exist, too, and prices are not low. Better-value premium Sauvignon sometimes comes from less well-known parts of the Loire – Quincy, Reuilly and Menetou-Salon, while for everyday quaffing, Sauvignon de Touraine and Vin de Pays du Jardin de la France Sauvignon Blanc (Loire 'country wines' made from this grape) can

hardly be bettered for simple, zesty refreshment at very reasonable prices. Further southwest, around the wider Bordeaux area, plenty of simple quaffing wines made from Sauvignon alone or Sauvignon and Sémillon are produced. The great oaked Bordeaux whites have no place in this section as they are certainly not light, but basic Bordeaux Blanc and whites from Bergerac and Entre-Deux-Mers provide a vast sea of Sauvignon of variable quality. A superior example is lemony and dry with a distinct note of freshly chopped grass. It would be wrong to generalise hugely about so much wine, but while most are palatable, south west Sauvignon doesn't tend to have the snappy, pure Sauvignon character that the Loire provides.

REST OF EUROPE

Austria is a source of fine Sauvignon, bracingly crisp and mouth-watering, the best of which is made in the Styria region to the south. Some

have startlingly high acidity, guaranteed to wake-up tired taste buds, although toned-down, less nervy wines, even some rich, oak-aged ones, have started to emerge more recently. Northern Italy is another important destination for the Sauvignon lover, the cool, high-altitude vineyards of the Friuli-Venezia-Guilia and Trentino-Alto Adige regions making simple, lean, racy Sauvignons that are refreshing but no more complex than that.

REST OF WORLD

Some lighter, crisper styles of Sauvignon are made in the coolest New World vineyards, such as Tasmania, Waipara/Canterbury in New Zealand, Casablanca Valley in Chile and Elgin in South Africa. These wines major on tangy citrus fruit rather than the richer, fruiter styles more generally seen in the New World (see pages 49-53).

OTHER LIGHT, DRY WHITES

PLENTY MORE TO PICK FROM

WELSCHRIESLING/ LASKI RIZLING

Don't make the mistake of thinking that all whites with Riesling/Rizling on the bottle are true Riesling. Welschriesling, aka Laski Rizling, has absolutely nothing to do with our fine German friend, and it makes much less exciting light, dry whites. These wines tend to be bland with a lower acidity (i.e. less refreshing) and they certainly don't age well, turning flat and dull within just a matter of months. A few palatable examples of Welschriesling come from Austria, but generally, this grape should be avoided in favour of real Riesling.

MUSCADET/MELON DE BOURGOGNE

Taste a poor Muscadet and you will probably start to wonder what all the fuss is about – it's simple, perhaps a little too tart, and frankly rather boring. Certainly nothing to write home about. The product of the area around Nantes in France's Loire Valley, this wine is a little overrated, although there are signs of a revival. But, still, there is a big jump in quality from basic Muscadet to the finest wines.

Premium Muscadet is aged on its yeast sediment (lees), which gives it a creamier edge, perhaps with a hint of fresh bread or even yoghurt, and in youth, a fresh prickle on the tongue of carbon dioxide gas. Quality is on the up in the Loire Valley and there are much better wines around now than there were only a decade ago. Look out for the words *sur lie* on a label. This will indicate a wine that has been bottled on the lees. Try to avoid the bargain basement examples here.

Melon de Bourgogne, by the way, is the real name for the grape that makes Muscadet. Good Muscadet is a decent wine for washing down seafood, especially oysters.

MÜLLER-THURGAU

This is the main grape behind many cheap, once-popular German whites that are now less fashionable: Hock, Liebfraumilch, Niersteiner and Piesporter. There's nothing inherently wrong with a clean, fresh example, but don't expect much. Müller-Thurgau has very little character compared with Riesling (which, ironically, is one of its parents – this is a modern cross between Riesling and a more obscure grape variety). It has hardly any fragrance or complexity, but growers love it as the vines flourish easily and produce loads of fruit. Plantings are in decline now, but it is still widely planted in Germany and it's a similar story in New Zealand: Müller-Thurgau was a major player here until recently, when other grapes started to prove more popular. Drinkers had simply discovered wines with better flavours and it fell from grace. It is just about possible to make a half-decent Müller-Thurgau, and a few

producers in New Zealand and Germany do so (as well as one or two in Italy and, believe it or not, England) but it takes a lot of care in the vineyard, and very low yields to make interesting wine.

PINOT GRIGIO AND OTHER ITALIAN WHITES

We're talking Pinot Grigio, Frascati, Soave and Orvieto here – a quartet of Italian whites that all taste light, clean, crisp and fresh. That's the idea, anyway. In reality there are too many oxidised and disappointing examples of all four around. The bland and characterless Trebbiano grape plays a major part in the production of Frascati, Soave and Orvieto. Cheap examples of these wines use mainly Trebbiano, while better bottles use higher proportions of a tastier grape such as Garganega in Soave. Pinot Grigio is the same as France's Pinot Gris grape, which makes rich and opulent wines in

Alsace, but light, lemony, sometimes spritzy whites in Italy. Try to find bottles that are fresh into the shop rather than those which have been hanging around collecting dust, as Pinot Grigio doesn't last well. And go for reputable producers – top Soave, say, from a fastidious winemaker, has bags more flavour than dirt-cheap, mass-produced Soave.

Frascati, Soave and Orvieto come from Lazio, Verona and Umbria, respectively. At their best, Frascati and Orvieto taste of fresh lemons with a hint of floral violet aroma. Soave can be more interesting, with creamier depths and a richer note of almond oil from a top producer (Pieropan is one name to look out for). Although these wines are more easily available, lesser-known whites from the central Marches region made from a grape called Verdicchio (this appears on the label) are more exciting: still fresh and snappy, but with a greater depth of limey flavour.

DRY MUSCAT

The Muscat family of related grape varieties is widespread, and many of the wines produced by its scions are sweet. But aromatic, dry Muscat is well worth a taste if you come across it. This is the only white wine that truly tastes of grapes above any other fruit – crunchy green grapes fresh from the fridge in the case of crisp, young, cold dry Muscat. As such it is a pretty, summery wine – perfect for hot days sitting in the garden, should any come our way! Dry Muscat is a speciality of Alsace in eastern France (try it with fresh asparagus) and there are a few great-value examples from Italy, Austria, Germany (where it is called Muskateller), and also Australia.

UGNI BLANC AND COLOMBARD

Colombard's roots are firmly in the Cognac region of France where it has been a mainstay of brandy production for centuries. One of the reasons it works so well in brandy is that the base wine it produces is neutral in character, so there you go – it makes pretty boring table wine. In the right hands, though, it can be fairly crisp and quaffable and it does have a light, floral edge. It is blended with Ugni Blanc to make the snappy, refreshing country wine Vin de Pays des Côtes de Gascogne and is also used for basic but palatable crisp whites in South Africa. Ugni Blanc is called Trebbiano in Italy (where it plays a major role in the Italian whites described above). It does not have enough natural character to create interesting wine.

GRÜNER VELTLINER

Austria's very own white grape makes distinctive wines with a clear note of white pepper twisted over racy citrus fruit. Not yet well-known overseas, Grüner Veltliner can produce strikingly good wines, wonderfully dry and lean yet full of flavour, and the best will even taste weighty and rich in texture, if tangy and succulent, and will age well for a couple of years. One to try if you fancy a change! Bründlmayer and Freie Weingärtner Wachau (FWW) are labels to sample.

ALIGOTÉ

Burgundy is famous for its world-beating Chardonnays (see pages 79–81), but another white grape also grows there. Aligoté is not nearly as important as Chardonnay in the region, and it doesn't create anything like such impressive wine, but as with many of the grapes described above, it makes a refreshing change. It generally produces wines that are tart and light, sometimes with a very slight spritz of gas, but ripe examples from a warm vintage can be a little creamier and fuller. Traditionally, this is the base wine for 'kir' – add a splash of crème de cassis (from Dijon if you want to be loyal to Burgundy!) to a glass of young, cold Aligoté for a wonderful summer aperitif.

STORING AND SERVING

SERVE THE LIGHT, DRY WHITES NICE AND COLD TO EMPHASISE THEIR REFRESHING, MOUTH-WATERING TANGINESS. Store in the fridge for at least an hour or two before serving, then keep the bottle cool by putting it on ice or back in the fridge. Serve in medium-sized white wine glasses (nothing too small or else you won't get the full benefits of those delicate aromas as you swirl the glass). A long-stemmed, elegant, plain glass is perfect for holding and looking at your wine. Very light, simple, dry whites need drinking up almost as soon as you buy them, as they will lose their fragile fragrance and fruit flavour very quickly. Good, crisp Sauvignon should stand up better for a few months, while a fine Riesling is surprisingly long-lived. Drink it up when young sometimes, but do try an older Riesling once in a while for a taste of honeyed apple, yet a dry finish, and even that famous hint of petrol on the aroma.

MAKING THE DIFFERENCE

LIGHT, DRY WHITES HAVE IMPROVED NO END IN QUALITY OVER THE PAST FIFTEEN YEARS OR SO; PUT SIMPLY, THEY ARE MORE RELIABLY FRESH, CLEAN AND CRISP THAN THEY USED TO BE. This is due partly to more sensitive handling of the grapes between picking and fermenting, so that subtle flavours are not lost, and partly to the use of low, controlled temperatures during fermentation. The wine is now usually fermented in stainless-steel tanks – much more hygienic than old-fashioned concrete vats. Indeed, hygiene is considered very important at wineries these days, and light, dry whites have benefitted hugely. There are still some oxidised, faded or plain grubby whites around, but fewer than ever before.

MATCHING LIGHT, DRY WHITES WITH FOOD

SUCCESSFUL FOOD-AND-WINE MATCHING IS ALL ABOUT BALANCING LIKE WITH LIKE OR, IN THIS CASE, LIGHT WITH LIGHT! Never match a tart, lean, dry white with very rich food or any form of red meat. Instead, these wines go well with crisp dishes such as tomato salad, grilled peppers and asparagus, and even stand up reasonably well to fruity or acidic salad dressings. They are great with white fish dishes, simple fresh seafood and, more surprisingly, they are good at washing down mild chicken and vegetable curries. Sauvignon Blanc is a wow with goat's cheese.

FIRST TASTE

■ If a light, dry white isn't refreshing, there's something seriously wrong with it! These wines are meant to be MOUTH-WATERING, PALATE-CLEANSING, TANGY AND CRISP, so reject any examples that taste flat and flabby – i.e.lacking in zesty fruit and acidity. They may be corked or just badly made, but they won't reach the spot!

■ TRY TO SAVOUR THE DELICATE AROMAS AND FLAVOURS. Even the most committed fan of full-on, ultra-fruity Chardonnay can learn to love their elegance and subtlety, if they take time to stop and notice the more restrained but often complex layers of scent and taste.

■ If you are bored with dull, light whites, TRY WINES MADE FROM PREMIUM GRAPE VARIETIES only and from top spots – Riesling from the Mosel in Germany, say, or Sauvignon Blanc from Sancerre in the Loire Valley. Avoid the cheapest wines from less interesting grapes.

■ Be aware that SOME LIGHT WHITES ARE MUCH DRIER THAN OTHERS. Some are medium and will taste distinctly sweet to those used to bracing, bone-dry whites. That doesn't necessarily mean they are poor quality, but they may not be to your taste. If you aren't sure what's in your bottle, TRY BEFORE YOU BUY.

BUYER'S GUIDE

■ Unless you are buying mature Riesling, aim to buy young, light whites. Bag the most recent vintage you can, and if the wine is non-vintage, check with the shop that it is a recent shipment. NEVER BUY LIGHT WHITES THAT HAVE BEEN SITTING AROUND TOO LONG, especially if they look dusty or the liquid has turned darker yellow.

■ SOME INEXPENSIVE FRENCH WINES IN THIS STYLE PROVIDE GOOD VALUE – young Vin de Pays des Côtes de Gascogne, or Sauvignon de Touraine, is heartwarmingly cheap, yet reliably fresh and appealing. Don't expect anything too exciting, though.

■ Further up the quality ladder, RIESLING CAN BE REMARKABLY CHEAP – partly as it has been out of fashion for a long time (except among wine aficionados, who have always loved it). Germany in particular offers some seriously good, light, white Riesling for little outlay.

■ THE CRISPEST, TANGIEST, MOST TANTALISINGLY SUBTLE, LIGHT WHITES COME FROM COOLER CLIMATES. Wines made in this style from hotter areas tend to taste bigger, riper and sometimes even oily – fine if you like that kind of thing, but not truly very 'light' and sometimes lacking finesse and subtlety.

MOVING ON

■ Germany and Austria make some of the best examples of light, dry whites, so DON'T BE PUT OFF BY THE OLD-FASHIONED GOTHIC SCRIPT AND SEEMINGLY DIFFICULT LABELS. The faint-hearted can always turn back to a boring big brand from Australia – be brave and give these hidden treasures a try!

■ Sample a fine German white wine and you will NEVER BUY THE CHEAP AND NASTY BOTTLES from the same country again. German wine is divided into the great and the gruesome – AVOID THE BLAND COMMERCIAL CHEAPIES.

■ VENTURE FURTHER AFIELD AND TRY LIGHT, DRY WHITES FROM UNUSUAL PLACES like Hungary, Austria, northern Italy and Switzerland, not just those from France and Germany.

■ Never try to pair the light, dry whites with very rich food – they will be overpowered by roast turkey and all the trimmings, or spicy sausages and gravy – so STICK TO LIGHT PARTNERS, OR SERVE THEM ALONE AS APERITIFS – these wines work just fine on their own.

FRUITY, SPICY WHITES **40**
69

IF YOU DON'T LIKE YOUR WHITES TOO PALLID AND WISHY-WASHY, BUT YOU HATE OAKY, POWERFUL WHITES, THEN LINGER OVER THE NEXT FEW PAGES. It can sometimes seem hard to locate those 'in-between' whites, as we all appear to be drowning in a sea of rich Chardonnay or weedy Liebfraumilch. Here, then, are the medium-bodied whites, many with ripe fruit and a heady perfume, but very few of them oaky. The wines that feature on these pages are either overtly fruity, packed with juicy, succulent flavour, like New Zealand Sauvignon Blanc, or they have a spicy hint, like Alsace Gewurztraminer. These wines have zoomed back into vogue of late, often replacing Chardonnay as a more refreshing type of white wine that still packs a punch. And as we shall see, they are also amazingly food-friendly, matching the most trendy dishes around.

You won't be impressed by everything that falls into this category. All styles of wine bring the odd let-down, and in the case of these, it usually comes in the form of a disappointingly dilute bottle which fails to deliver a loud blast of character. Or it can be because the wine is too flabby; it lacks firm acidity to give a fresh streak to all that fruit and spice. Then there is the level of sweetness – often a tricky problem with white wine. A bone-dry glass is expected but instead you get something faintly sugary – or vice versa. The good news is that most modern producers make crisp, dry wines and in the case of Alsace, you can easily avoid the very sweet wines. Then again, the medium wines can be so wonderful that you may not even mind that honeyed tinge.

APPEARANCE

Straw-coloured, heading towards gold hints, sometimes a little green. Not as pale as the light whites, but less richly coloured than heavily oaked or many sweet wines.

TEXTURE

Medium – not exactly viscous, but not nearly as thin as the light whites.

FLAVOUR

Lots of interesting nuances similar to those found on the scent, although good fresh fruit should be at the core. Should have a clean, crisp finish.

AROMA

Terrific! Fruity whites have citrus or tropical fruits or apple leaping out of the glass. Grass, green pepper, even tomato leaves can be found, too. Sauvignon Blanc can be very pungent, with ripe gooseberry, asparagus and even a hint of tom-cat or sweat. Spicy whites have a heady, exotic perfume. A scent of roses is often found, along with cake spices (nutmeg, ginger), lychees… even Turkish delight.

SAUVIGNON BLANC

REFRESHING, RACY, AROMATIC

More and more of us are waking up to the joys of Sauvignon Blanc in all its manifestations. A few years ago Chardonnay seemed to be everywhere and the only famous and popular style of Sauvignon Blanc was Sancerre. Now Sauvignon (you don't need to say 'blanc' all the time) has stepped out from Chardonnay's shadow and become a fashionable grape variety sourced from many countries. It's well-loved partly because it offers a different, racier, leaner mouthful than Chardonnay, and partly because it's rarely barrel-aged, so it appeals to those who dislike oak. But be aware: there's a wide range of Sauvignon out there.

Some of the most famous wines made from this variety, like the Sauvignons from the cool Loire Valley in France, are distinctly subtle and elegant, and as such, they were dealt with in the first section of this book, along with the bracingly fresh and light Sauvignons of Austria and northern Italy (see pages 22-5). Although these wines have a certain clean, lemony quality, they could not be described as fruit-driven and ripe. Anyone who has tried a Sauvignon Blanc from the southern hemisphere however, will know that these are more extrovert wines. Most warm-climate Sauvignons are ultra-fruity, richly aromatic and packed with bright, vivacious perfume and flavour. There are plenty of Sauvignons that hover between the reserved French and the louder New Zealand styles, but generally speaking, most New World examples fall firmly into the fruity category. And these are the wines that have woken up the modern world to Sauvignon Blanc and just what a refreshing thrill it can provide.

NEW ZEALAND
New Zealand's wines weren't famous for anything much until Marlborough Sauvignon Blanc hit the scene. Back in the seventies, this was a

winemaking country that turned out some reasonable whites but that didn't wow the critics. The beautiful, cool, Marlborough region in the South Island was mainly covered in fields and sheep, not vines. Then something remarkable happened. A couple of wineries thought it would be a great idea to plant the Sauvignon Blanc grape – best known for making decent dry whites in France's Loire Valley and Bordeaux region – in the stony, well-drained soils of Marlborough's valleys. They reckoned that the low night-time temperatures there and the long, gradual ripening season, as well as that rocky terrain, might just produce decent white wine from this grape. And they were right.

It's still hard to believe that Marlborough Sauvignon only hit our shop shelves in the eighties. It seems like a style of wine that has always been there – a classic. Although it is still a newcomer (compared to Sancerre, Bordeaux Sauvignon and Pouilly-Fumé) that is exactly what it has become: a modern classic, a new type of white wine made by planting a traditional French grape variety in a totally different part of the world. The Sauvignon from this little corner of a small island in the Antipodes took everyone by storm. From the very first sniff of crunchy, fresh gooseberries to the underlying hints of tomato leaf, herbs, grass, tom-cat (yes, really, but it's not as bad as it sounds), asparagus and passion-fruit, New Zealand Sauvignon is utterly distinctive.

It's possible to get bored with that relentless, rather over-the-top, pungent gooseberry character, but most wine-lovers return to New Zealand Sauvignon sooner or later for a reminder of just how vibrant and bright white wine can be. It's a great antidote to dull, insipid whites (of which far too many examples still exist). Ring the changes to some extent by trying examples from other parts of New Zealand. Although Marlborough still remains the most important region for Sauvignon (many, many wineries now make it there and the sheep have had to find new pastures), other spots on both islands do well with this grape, too. Still on the South Island, the regions of Nelson near Marlborough and Waipara/Canterbury near the town of Christchurch, are important sources of Sauvignon (expect a slightly leaner, crisper character from Canterbury), while on the North Island, Martinborough (or Wairarapa, as it is known) is the source of some very impressive, savoury and rich Sauvignon.

Don't stick to just one winery, either, even if it is a fashionable label. There are plenty of quality wines to choose from, so taste around New Zealand Sauvignon. A few Sauvignons have a small amount of Sémillon in the blend; others are made with a proportion aged in oak for a short time, for a subtle roundness; still more are deliberately turned out lean, herbaceous and grassy. The most famous New Zealand wine of all, the cultish Cloudy Bay Sauvignon Blanc, is still on fine form, though it can be horribly expensive to buy in restaurants. Some of the cheaper New Zealand Sauvignons offer better value for money, for example Villa Maria's Private Bin, Montana's range and Babich.

SOUTH AFRICA

South Africa is going great guns with Sauvignon at the moment. Although the Cape's wine industry fell behind the rest of the world during the dark days of apartheid, there is now a new sense of excitement about South African wine, and Sauvignon is emerging as one of the most successful white grapes of the modern era. The style of modern Cape Sauvignon falls somewhere between the elegance of the Loire wines and the richer fruitiness of New Zealand – perfect for drinkers who find one too restrained and the other too overtly pungent. Tasters may notice an attractive lime and passion-fruit streak and possibly a hint of green capsicum, rather than the gooseberry and "tom-cat" of New Zealand Sauvignon. Exciting wine is now being made in several parts of the Western Cape, including the Robertson and Constantia regions. Good brands to try: Springfield, Klein Constantia and Vergelegen.

CHILE

Unfortunately, it's not always possible to know when you are getting true Sauvignon Blanc from Chile, despite what's on the label. The problem is that many of Chile's Sauvignon vineyards have been found to contain a quite different variety called Sauvignonasse, which tastes similar when first made but tires quickly, growing fruitless and flat in flavour. That said, a reputable winery should be providing one hundred percent Sauvignon Blanc, and some Chilean examples are delicious, bone-dry and zippily fresh, with crisp gooseberry and lime and occasionally a slight savoury edge. The cool Casablanca Valley region makes some of the best. Go for Viña Casablanca or the good-value 35 South and Miguel Torres labels.

AUSTRALIA

This is not a grape variety at which Australia excels. Winemakers there have tended to concentrate on Chardonnay and Sémillon, leaving Sauvignon to their Kiwi neighbours. It is partly because many of Australia's top vineyard sites are simply too hot for Sauvignon, which needs a cooler touch if it is to remain racy and crisp. Still, the Australians are now looking to make more elegant wines alongside their traditional blockbusters, and so Sauvignon has become much more popular among winemakers as they plant in cooler spots. The result is some impressive stuff, especially from Adelaide Hills, Tasmania and the Margaret River region south of Perth (where it is sometimes blended with Semillon). Examples to try: Knappstein Lenswood, Katnook or Cullen's blend with Semillon.

USA

The Californians have developed a unique type of Sauvignon and called it Fumé Blanc. This is oaked Sauvignon – so expect more richness, some creamy depths and sometimes a sweet note that will not be to everyone's taste. West Coast winemakers who first pushed this style had fine, oaked white Bordeaux in mind; unfortunately, too many Fumé Blancs lacked zippy acidity, dryness and the fruity stamp of Sauvignon. The style has been toned down of late – more of that bright, lively Sauvignon character is allowed to shine through, and there are certain Californian winemakers

who don't use oak barrels at all for Sauvignon. But do tread carefully here until you establish that you like the Californian style! Washington State is the source of a few fruity, modern Sauvignons, too.

REST OF EUROPE

Bulgaria produces some reasonable Sauvignon Blanc, though overall quality is quite patchy. Hungary tends to be a safer bet. This is a country which makes some super Sauvignon: dry, fresh, flavoursome and cheap, with tangy grapefruit and an often rather savoury, smoky note. It is great for everyday quaffing. The south of France makes some Sauvignon in a richer, riper style than usual – the warm vineyards account for this.

GEWÜRZTRAMINER

SOMETHING QUITE DIFFERENT

It's hard to explain what the much-used term 'spicy white' means, but grab a glass of Gewürztraminer (or "Gewürz", as this grape is often called) and the style immediately becomes clear. It's not hot, peppery chilli spice, of course, but an exotic, gingery appeal, with hints of peach skin, rosewater, dried apricots, sometimes a note of cardamom and often pink Turkish delight. Good Gewürz is headily perfumed, so the extraordinary, unique appeal of the wine assails you long before you get the liquid in your mouth. One sniff of a glass of Gewürz will tell you that here is something quite different.

To be honest, it isn't for everyone, and even for its fans it probably isn't an everyday quaffer – but Gewürz is fascinating stuff, and like all the spicy whites, it's a brilliant match for certain dishes; in this case I'd choose Thai spicy fish with lots of coriander and lemongrass, or even simple Chinese sweet-and-sour chicken.

ALSACE AND THE REST OF EUROPE

The most famous and best Gewurztraminers of all come from Alsace in eastern France – a region that has mastered premium, opulent but unoaked whites. These wines are full of fragrance and spice, richly golden-coloured and full in texture, often with a high thirteen percent alcohol, but they are not oaky, and a well-balanced example (as always with whites) should have crisp acidity to balance out that weight.

Wines from over fifty *grand cru* vineyard sites (named on the label) are supposed to be the best, but this isn't always the case and such bottles can be an expensive disappointment. Avoiding sweetish wines (or finding them, if you like a more honeyed style) can also prove tricky as there's little to help you on the label, but note that the words *vendange tardive* or *sélection des grains nobles* do indicate sweet wine. Poor Alsace

Gewurz does exist, of course, often tasting 'flabby', lacking acidity and smelling like cheap perfume. Avoid this by picking top producers like Hugel, Trimbach or Schlumberger or try a simpler but less expensive wine from a reliable cooperative winery like Turckheim or Ribeauvillé. Despite these pitfalls – and the fact that Alsace Gewurz is often packaged in old-fashioned tall, green bottles with dense Gothic script on them – do give it a go as the wines can be quite brilliant, and among the most unusual and fascinating in the world.

In Germany, Gewürztraminer is considered much less important than Riesling. The wines are simpler, but prettily scented and often delicious. The best have a delightfully crisp finish; the worst taste clumsy and unbalanced. Try a bottle from the Baden or Pfalz areas of the country. If you like Gewürz, trawl the shelves for bottles from Eastern Europe (especially Hungary) and northern Italy – these can be a bargain and snappily fresh, although nothing touches Alsace Gewurz.

REST OF THE WORLD

New Zealand produces some tasty Gewurztraminer, especially from the cooler vineyards of Marlborough. There's a delightful purity of fruit here – a clean citrus zest, tangerine note, perhaps some lychee – and a dry, mineral quality to the best. Australia makes very few Gewurzes of note as its vineyards are usually too hot for this variety, although cool, breezy Tasmania can produce a subtle, elegant wine. Chilean Gewurz, on the other hand, is successful, especially from the cool Casablanca Valley vineyards or the Bío-Bío region in the south. There aren't many around, but snap one up from Undurraga, Cono Sur, or Viña Casablanca if you spot it. This doesn't crop up much in California, but a handful of decent wines come from Washington State.

OTHER FRUITY, SPICY WHITES

PLENTY MORE TO PICK FROM

CHENIN BLANC

Drinkers of fruity, spicy whites usually like Chenin Blanc – when it's good, that is. This a difficult grape variety to fall in love with, partly because one of the two countries that makes a lot of it – South Africa – turns out so much commercial, off-dry wine from Chenin.

It's worth persevering with South African Chenin Blanc (sometimes known locally as Steen), though, as a superior bottle has a lovely juiciness to it, with plenty of lime and guava flavours, a nice rounded weight and a succulent finish. The better examples of South African Chenins are moreish, crowd-pleasing wines, reasonably cheap and great party whites. Happily, the general standard is improving, and even supermarket own-labels are proving to be more reliable. Among the best producers are Mulderbosch (lightly oaked wine), Ken Forrester and Spier.

In France's Loire Valley, Chenin gets serious. This is where the amazingly long-lived Savennières is made entirely from Chenin; rapier-sharp with acidity when young, it achingly slowly evolves into richer stuff with layers of ripe apple and cream over ten or twenty years in the cellar. Vouvray, too, can show Chenin Blanc at its best, with appley fruit again, and a subtle hint of walnut oil (Vouvray can be dry, medium or sweet). Be warned though that basic Loire whites made from this grape can be a real let-down. Humble Anjou Blanc is often over-sulphured and dilute in flavour, with a faint, wet-wool aroma, like a jumper that has been left out in the rain!

To be fair to this grape, it is able to produce some impressive white wines when in the hands of a canny producer (Huët or Nicolas Joly) and it's also a versatile beast, creating good examples of tasty sparkling and luscious sweet wines.

PINOT BLANC

It's hard to find anyone who actively dislikes Pinot Blanc. This grape produces wines which are easy to drink, soft, fairly fruity in an appley sort of way, sometimes with a creamy quality and a note of almond oil or peach kernel. It is as a food wine that Pinot Blanc comes into its own, slipping down effortlessly with a wide range of savoury dishes. If you are dining in a crowd and aren't sure which white wine to choose, opt for Pinot Blanc. In Alsace, where arguably the best Pinot Blanc is made, the wine is served with onion tart. The soft, almost earthy wine combined with highly flavoured vegetable or egg dishes works very well.

ALBARIÑO

Spain is much more famous for its fine red wines (from Rioja, and more recently Ribera and Navarra) than it is for its whites, which at the cheaper end of the market can be decidedly plonk-like. But one serious white is made in the western extremes of the country. The Rías Baixas region of Galicia, on the Atlantic coast, is the source of a lovely dry white. Oozing succulent, ripe orange and lime juice, Albariño has good rich weight, crisp acidity and no oak. Well chilled, it is a star match for white fish dishes.

MORIO-MUSKAT AND IRSAI OLIVER

These are the also-rans among spicy whites – after Gewürztraminer, that is. You won't get the depth of flavour or sheer excitement of an Alsace Gewurz here, but you should get something of that rosewater, lychee and ginger exoticism, and a crisp, fresh finish. Prices are low for both, so these grapes make an acceptable introduction to the spicy white style. Morio-Muskat, which majors on the floral, scented character, is usually from Germany, while Irsai Oliver, which is usually snappy and dry with spicy peach flavour, hails from Slovenia or Hungary.

STORING AND SERVING

THE MAJORITY OF THE FRUITY, SPICY WHITES NEED DRINKING UP SOON AFTER PURCHASE, AS THEIR WONDERFUL AROMAS AND VIBRANT FLAVOURS WON'T LAST MORE THAN A YEAR. This applies especially to the more cheap and simple bottles like basic Irsai Oliver. New Zealand Sauvignon is supposed to be consumed fairly young, but older bottles have proved delicious: full of tinned asparagus and baked greengage character. Cellar a top example, but drink up leaner, lesser wines within a year. Albariño and Pinot Blanc aren't great 'agers', either, so enjoy them while they're fairly young. But serious Alsace Gewurztraminer can be matured successfully for much longer – several years in bottle gives it a lovely mellow richness – although be warned that the blast of spice softens somewhat. This is one wine that can be enjoyed young or old, according to your taste.

MAKING THE DIFFERENCE

THE BEST SAUVIGNON BLANC IS GROWN IN RELATIVELY COOL-CLIMATE VINEYARDS, SO THE GRAPES RETAIN THEIR CRISP ACIDITY AND MOUTH-WATERING FRUIT FLAVOURS, RATHER THAN TURNING FLABBY AND OILY. But cool climates bring another potential problem: lack of ripeness, especially as Sauvignon is a vigorous vine which tends to send a vast green canopy over the grapes, shading them from the sun. One answer to this is canopy management, when the leaves are cut back to expose the grapes to sunlight and air. By using careful canopy management, growers can achieve sufficient ripeness without having to replant in warmer areas. In an area famous for Sauvignon, like Marlborough in New Zealand, the bright daytime sunshine and colder night-time temperatures bring about well-balanced grapes with intense fruit flavours as well as crisp acidity.

MATCHING FRUITY, SPICY WHITES WITH FOOD

THE FRUITY, SPICY WHITES DESCRIBED HERE ARE NEITHER TOO OVERPOWERING ON ONE HAND, NOR WIMPY ON THE OTHER, SO THEY MATCH A WIDE RANGE OF DISHES, INCLUDING SIMPLE CHICKEN AND FISH. Pinot Blanc, for example, goes with lots of dishes, especially quiches, tarts and pizzas. The richer, fruity Sauvignons are great with asparagus, tomato and basil salad, and rich white fish and seafood dishes (fish in creamy sauce, fresh crab). Albariño is a wow with firm white fish, especially the hake often served in western Spain. Spicy whites are the ones to match with more exotic food – Gewürztraminer with mildly spicy, fragrant Thai dishes, or Chinese cuisine. Try a ultra-fruity Sauvignon or Gewürz with rich cheesy bakes or roast vegetables, as they both measure up well to hearty vegetarian fare.

FIRST TASTE

■ Sauvignon from the Loire Valley in France tastes much leaner than rich, ripe New Zealand Sauvignon, and South African styles sit somewhere in between. MAKE SURE YOU KNOW WHERE YOUR SAUVIGNON COMES FROM. Don't expect them all to taste the same because they are from the same grape variety – Sauvignons vary a lot.

■ Often called Fumé Blanc, OAKED U.S. SAUVIGNON HAS AN ALMOST SWEET, VANILLA NOTE AND WILL BE RICHER AND OFTEN LESS CRISP. Fine, if you like that sort of thing, but be aware of it. White Bordeaux is sometimes oaky, too.

■ Not everyone likes Gewürztraminer; PEOPLE TEND EITHER TO LOVE OR LOATHE THE FRUITY, SPICY WHITES. So it's a good idea to pick something else if you are trying to please a crowd.

■ Do try these wines with food, and not just on their own, as THESE ARE THE MOST CONSUMMATELY FOOD-FRIENDLY OF ALL THE WHITE WINES.

BUYER'S GUIDE

■ YOU DON'T HAVE TO SPEND A FORTUNE TO GET A DECENT FRUITY, SPICY WHITE. Trade up from the very cheapest and you'll hit a reasonably low price bracket where plenty of tangy, succulent flavour is delivered, particularly from the Sauvignon Blanc grape.

■ It may cost a little more, but as long as you avoid the cult labels, NEW ZEALAND SAUVIGNON CAN BE GOOD VALUE WITH LOADS OF FLAVOUR, and is a reliable type of wine.

■ Very cheap Gewürztraminer is worth avoiding – this is where the grape starts to smell and taste like floral air freshener! Hungary makes some bargain bottles of Gewurz; however, IT'S DEFINITELY WORTH SPLASHING OUT ON THE BEST GEWURZTRAMINER FROM ALSACE once in a while.

■ CHENIN BLANC FROM SOUTH AFRICA IS A SAFE BET FOR A PARTY WHITE – it is cheap, reliably tasty and fun, if pretty simple stuff. Poor examples from the Loire abound, but try a fine one from a top producer for a treat sometime, and discover Chenin at its best.

MOVING ON

■ IF YOU LOVE NEW ZEALAND SAUVIGNON, TRY OTHER WINES FROM DIFFERENT PARTS OF THIS COUNTRY. Most Sauvignon comes from Marlborough, but sample others from the Martinborough, Central Otago and Canterbury regions, too.

■ TRY BLENDS OF SAUVIGNON WITH SÉMILLON, as seen a great deal in the southwest of France. Most white Bordeaux is a blend of the two, and the pairing of these two grapes can be sensational.

■ Like Gewürztraminer? TRY OTHER FRUITY, SPICY WHITES – they are much more obscure but fascinating nonetheless. Irsai Oliver and Morio-Muskat should be on your shopping list.

■ Rather than finding a wine to complement a dish, MAKE SOME FOOD ESPECIALLY TO SHOW OFF YOUR FRUITY, SPICY WHITES. These wines are fantastically good with Thai and Chinese dishes, so dig out your wok and make a dish to match Gewürz.

FEW PEOPLE SIT ON THE FENCE WHEN IT COMES TO RIPE, FULL-BODIED WHITE WINES. Some love them, revelling in their powerful flavours and rich textures, while others prefer their whites light and refreshing. Then there is the issue of oak-ageing. Some heavyweight white wines never see the inside of a barrel, but many spend a long period maturing (and sometimes fermenting, too) in casks, becoming even more strongly flavoured as a result of the toasted oaky character leaching into the wine. Opinion will always be divided, but winemakers who are careful to balance the fruit, acid and oak elements so that nothing is overwhelming or out of kilter should always win the most fans.

Ten years ago, robust, hefty whites were all the rage. Wine-drinkers had grown tired of dilute, wimpy whites and the bright, fruit-driven styles arriving from warm vineyards in Australia and California were a welcome shock to the senses.

Suddenly here were white wines bursting with generous, plump fruit and dripping with creamy oak. Then the inevitable backlash followed - we had had enough of these extroverts and longed for something more subtle. Nowadays there are rich whites with (generally) better balance, more elegant flavours and crisper acidity to counteract those bold, 'in-yer-face' fruit and oak flavours.

The key to enjoying richer whites is to open them at the right moment. Blockbuster Chardonnays and Viogniers are not meant to be quaffed as crisp, light lunchtime aperitifs. But they stand up well to food, making brilliant partners for luxury dishes such as smoked salmon pâté, lobster or even roast turkey and all the trimmings. By contrast, a thin, weedy white would be totally overpowered by these dishes. Hearty food, luxury feasts and cold weather all make us want fleshier, richer wines. So if any white wines can be described as winter warmers, these are the ones!

TEXTURE

Relatively rich and weighty, more viscous than the lighter whites, less so than the sweet whites.

APPEARANCE

Bright yellow, hay-coloured; deeper in colour than the lighter whites with golden glints.

FLAVOUR

Full and fruity, fairly viscous and weighty in texture for a dry white. Fruit flavours include ripe oranges, peaches, apricots, pineapples and mangos. Buttery, creamy undertones, occasionally a distinct nuttiness. Lightly oaked wines have subtle roundness and a layer of vanilla; heavily oaked ones carry more toasty, sawdusty character. Some older wines take on a honeyed, bees-wax note while remaining dry. Lingering, full after-taste.

AROMA

Richly perfumed with hints of vanilla, cream, rich fruit (especially pineapples and peaches) perhaps buttered toast and hints of spicy wood from fermenting and/or ageing in oak barrels. Some (e.g. Viognier) have a heavy floral, honeysuckle-and-lilies perfume.

CHARDONNAY

RICH, RIPE AND POWERFUL

For many people, rich, ripe and powerful white wine means only one thing: the Chardonnay grape. Take top-quality Chardonnay grapes and ferment them in new-oak barrels, leaving the wine to age there awhile, and the result can be a supremely sophisticated and complex wine, for many the most exciting white wine in the world. And it packs a flavoursome punch.

Chardonnay does occasionally produce light, bland wine, but not often – that's one reason why winemakers across the globe like growing it so much. That, and the fact that they can mould it any way they like, as Chardonnay is easy to work with (it grows well and likes oak-ageing, for example). With plenty of ripe citrus and tropical fruit, tempting notes of toasted hazelnuts, peach kernels, buttered brioche and cream, top examples are some of the most satisfying and wonderful whites ever made.

FRANCE

To taste the very best, splash out on a fine example from the Burgundy region of France. White Burgundy is almost always made from Chardonnay, although it won't say so on the label – as in many French classic wine regions, the Burgundians don't advertise their grape varieties, instead focussing on the village or individual vineyard where the wine was made. Other white grapes like Aligoté, Pinot Blanc and Pinot Gris are also grown in Burgundy, but these are relative rarities; you can be certain that if you buy mainstream white Burgundy you are getting a bottle of one hundred percent Chardonnay.

Indeed, if you splash out on some of the premium wines that come from Burgundy's prize locations along the Côte d'Or – most come from the the southern Côte de Beaune area between Aloxe-Corton and Santenay – you should see what first-rate Chardonnay can achieve: opulent, remarkably concentrated, yet also beautifully fresh and well-balanced wine, the oaky hints enhancing, not overpowering, that gorgeous, mouth-filling, honeyed-yet-dry fruit. Wines to try – and don't forget these names refer to the location not the producer or grape variety – include those from the villages of Meursault, Chassagne-Montrachet, Puligny-Montrachet, Aloxe-Corton, with first-rate vineyard areas including Corton-Charlemagne, Le Montrachet and Bâtard-Montrachet. The best bottles age well, too, losing any hard edges and mellowing to become wonderfully well-knit, the softer acidity and fruit binding seamlessly with the nutty, creamy oak.

Or that's the idea, anyway. Burgundy is a frustratingly difficult and patchy wine region, with big differences between fine and poor vintages, and plenty of inferior wine as well as those true stars. Even Burgundy connoisseurs acknowledge that

quality can be uneven, for whites as well as reds. Since the best wines are so expensive, it's important to pick a top producer and mug up on the good years. For the record, 1997, 1999, and 2000 through to 2004 were all good. Try to spend a bit extra now and again and sample pricier white burgundy, as it only gets great once it gets expensive. This is partly because all the top vineyards (classified as *grands crus*, the great growths – the top spots – followed by the *premiers crus* areas) can only produce a small amount of wine, and international demand for it is, of course, very high. But these are wines well worth saving up for.

Trawl around the cheaper white burgundies and, sadly, you will be in for a few disappointments, especially if you have sampled the great and glorious of the region. Those from the Côte Chalonnais, such as Rully, Montagny and Mercurey, can be reasonably good value, offering fresh, quality white at a less-scary price than the Côte d'Or. But Chardonnays from the vast vineyards of the Mâconnais area can be very unreliable; basic Mâcon Blanc in particular is a dodgy way to part with your money and can taste thin and raw. Do try burgundies labelled Pouilly-Fuissé, though, from a superior part of the Mâcon – they are often satisfyingly creamy and rich, and St-Véran provides some decent, good-value stuff in the mid-price bracket. Even basic, generic Bourgogne Blanc from a top winemaker can be surprisingly good: fresh, fruity, juicy and ripe.

Chablis, a famous white-wine area to the north of the Burgundy region, traditionally makes wine that is lighter in style, partly because it has slightly cooler vineyards. In some parts of Chablis, the soil is rich in chalk and clay, and traditionalists believe the best wines are made from Chardonnay grown on these sites (the soil is known as Kimmeridgian). Chablis is often described as having a steely quality – it certainly tastes a little leaner, more crisp, even with a more mineral edge, than other white burgundies. It is also more lightly oaked, even sometimes unoaked. As such, it perhaps belongs in our fruity whites section – except that in recent times more rich and rounded, ultra-fruity Chablis has been appearing. Expect warm, tangy hints of apple, orange and even rhubarb. This wine is not a true heavyweight, then, but rather represents the lighter face of Chardonnay, albeit with that characteristically generous fruit. Pick a Chablis from one of the *grands crus* (great growths, see page 20) of the region – Blanchots, Bougros, Les Clos, Grenouilles, Preuses, Valmur, Vaudésir – or from one of the more numerous *premiers crus*, the next step down. Quality in Chablis, by the way, is thankfully more reliable than in other parts of Burgundy.

For simpler joys, with less chance of disappointment but admittedly fewer high points, try Chardonnays from other parts of France. In particular, fans of rich, oaky whites won't want to miss the buttery, generous Chardonnays of the deep south of France. These wines (often labelled Vins de Pays d'Oc, country wines of the Languedoc), really do seem to taste sunny, exuding the warmth of the Southern vineyards, which creates super-ripe Chardonnay grapes. But they are 'identikit' wines, tasting very similar to one another and hardly reflecting *terroir* (the character of an individual site) in the same way decent burgundy does.

Most of these southern belles are aged in oak barrels or by using oak chips. A few are blends, but mostly they are one hundred percent Chardonnay. You know what you are getting here; not only is it much more likely to say Chardonnay on the label, but you can pretty much guarantee succulent pineapple and peachiness, buttery-toasty hints, and a rich, satisfyingly full finish. They are much more reliable than basic white burgundy, but don't expect great complexity or excitement. They taste a lot like Chardonnay from newer wine-making countries – one reason why the south of France has been dubbed the 'New, New World'.

AUSTRALIA

Which brings us to the second most famous Chardonnay-producing country in the world. Down Under, in Australia's warm vineyards, an ultra-rich, wonderfully concentrated, luxuriously ripe form of Chardonnay has proved extremely popular around the world. It used to be almost too much, leaving you with a mouthful of sawdust and vanilla. 'Blockbuster' was the word used to describe the heftiest, chunkiest Australian Chardonnays from hot areas like Hunter Valley in New South Wales, and the Barossa Valley near Adelaide.

These wines wowed us on first taste (they first arrived in significant numbers in the 1980s). If you had only ever sipped bland, weak, light white wines such as poor Muscadet and Liebfraumilch, Australian Chardonnay was a shock to the senses. What a blast of ripe, tropical fruit! What a rich perfume! What a dollop of vanilla and spice from all that fresh, resinous new oak! The problem is, like most extroverts, the loudest wines get a bit tiresome after a while. They are so heavy and gloopy, it's as though you should scoop them up with a spoon, not knock them back at a party. Recently the Aussies have started to make slightly more elegant wines. They age them in oak for a briefer period, or use older, less resinous oak, or they don't use wood at all, making their wines entirely in stainless-steel containers. Sometimes they source their grapes from cooler sites where the flavours don't get so overblown and where the acidity has more bite.

Among the cool-climate areas to look out for (helpfully, the Australians spell these out on a label) are the island of Tasmania, off the south coast of the mainland, the Adelaide Hills and Clare Valley regions in South Australia, and Mornington Peninsula and Yarra Valley in Victoria. Expect wines from these areas to taste more crisp and elegant than wines from warmer spots, although, with the exception of the ultra-fresh Tassie wines, they still retain plenty of broad, ripe Aussie fruit. Top producers include Petaluma, Knappstein Lenswood, Tarrawarra and Grosset. But despite the rise of such relatively cool-climate wines, baking-hot regions such as the Barossa Valley and Hunter Valley are still putting out heftier, chunkier styles, and the Margaret River in Western Australia is coming up with a refined Chardonnay style that lies somewhere in between. Try the Cullen, Leeuwin Estate or Cape Mentelle labels from the latter.

Despite these advances, some very rich Australian Chardonnays are still around, and they are great with food such as the most luxurious lobster, the creamiest fish sauces, smoked salmon or roast turkey. But they're too much on their own as aperitifs. The new lighter styles (still big, but not *so* big) are fresher, more balanced more thirst-quenching, more restrained. The latest trend is towards regional characteristics, Burgundy-style, so watch out for marked differences in wines from the far-flung Aussie wine regions. Try a few to see which suits you best.

Blends of Chardonnay with the Sémillon grape are common in Australia. These are no great shakes, almost seeming like simpler, 'dumb-blonde' versions of the straight Chardonnays. But they are generally clean, bright and have enough of that sunny fruit. Prices are pretty low too. Appealing crowd-pleasers, they usually go down well at a party.

REST OF WORLD

In California, it has been a similar story with Chardonnay. The West Coast winemakers used to make hugely successful, monster Chardonnay that you could almost cut with a knife, but they are now turning to a more subtle style and growing grapes in cooler vineyard areas for more restrained flavours and fresher streaks of acidity. The best examples now rival anything made in France and Australia, although they are mightily expensive.

At the cheaper end, California Chardonnay can taste a bit over-oaky, sweet and bland. Not really to everyone's taste, especially if you are used to drinking more sophisticated fare! In between lie some impressive Chardonnays, fairly full-on in character and also heavily oaked, but better balanced by riper flavours of concentrated pineapple and peach, and a crisp finish. And do splash out on premium West Coast wines once in a while – they are sublime, they age well for years, and are a must for those who love big whites. Try examples from the Carneros region, Russian River or the Sonoma Coast for poised, balanced bottles. Top names include Au Bon Climat, Beringer, Saintsbury, Kistler, and Hess. Avoid big, inexpensive brands.

South Africa is rapidly improving, making newly impressive Chardonnays. The Western Cape's wineries, which fell behind the times during apartheid and an estranged overseas market, have been a long time catching up, but today anyone who is a fan of the upfront and oaky style of white wine should give Cape Chardonnay a go – look for ones from the Robertson, Stellenbosch and Paarl regions for a taste of the best. These wines are typically rich and no-nonsense examples, but with well-controlled, rounded oak structure.

New Zealand is another source of fine Chardonnay. Its warmer areas (Gisborne and Hawke's Bay on the North Island) produce richer wines with a tropical-fruit edge; the cooler spots like Marlborough on the South Island, make a crisper, more citric version, but they are all typically packed with a juicy, pure flavour. Perhaps because of the fame of New Zealand's Sauvignon Blanc, its Chardonnay has often been forgotten in the rush, so don't miss out. Some of the most important wineries (Villa Maria, Te Mata, Sileni, Palliser, Hunter's, Cloudy Bay) make excellent Chardonnays. Try to sample wines from different regions, including Martinborough on the North Island and Central Otago on the South, if you can.

Then there's South America, and Chile, origin of so much good-value Chardonnay. If you want lots of fruit for your money, and a reliable source of fresh, clean white with a nicely judged edge of oak, give Chilean Chardonnay a whirl. There are a few super-premium, more pricey Chilean wines around, too, which prove that the country can make top stuff. And go for the new kid on the Chardonnay block: Argentina, now impressing us with its new, highly modern, bright and big Chardonnays at heart-warmingly low prices.

Don't be fooled into thinking that Europe's sole Chardonnay stronghold is France – even though the shop shelves are groaning with French examples. In fact, if you like plump, rich Chardonnay, you should look into the bastion of good-value bottles that is Eastern Europe. Bulgaria and Hungary both turn out reasonably good, clean and tasty versions; nothing very special, but since they are cheap, they're fine for everyday quaffing. Don't expect anything fantastically rich and powerful, however. Soft, fruity and simple is the name of the game here. In Italy,

however, things get more serious with the richly oaked premium wines made in Tuscany, and the highly modern, Aussie taste-alikes from the hot vineyards of Sicily. Spain and Portugal major in other styles of wine, but there are still a number of well-made, almost-serious, oaked Chardonnays about. One surprising source of high-class, judiciously oaked Chardonnay is Austria. The Austrians sometimes call this grape Morillon, and best examples come from the Wachau and Styria regions. These little-known gems are a rarity on the export market – so if you see one, snap it up! Even rarer outside its country of origin is Canadian Chardonnay but that, too, can be serious stuff with incisive acidity to balance the richness. And if you see one of China's buttery, oaked Chardonnays, give it a whirl; a small handful is now being exported, appearing mainly in Chinese restaurants worldwide – expect more in due course.

SÉMILLON

A VERSATILE BEAST

Produce of Australia

SEMILLON
CHARDONNAY

South Eastern Australia

2001

Sometimes blended with Chardonnay to create limey, buttery, rounded white wines, Sémillon deserves its own listing for the weighty, toasty, almost smoky wines made from it in newer wine-making countries. Sémillon is a chameleon-like grape. Sometimes it makes lean, grassy whites that would be out of place in this style section, but when it's ripe, mature and sometimes oak-aged, it certainly falls into the 'rich whites' category. Then it makes just about the best dessert wines in the world as well. A versatile beast, then.

AUSTRALIA AND REST OF THE WORLD

If it's big and loud, 'in-yer-face' Semillon you're after, head to Australia – in particular the Hunter Valley (NSW) and the Clare and Barossa Valleys (South Australia) for sun-baked, so-ripe-they're-almost-sweet wines which are packed with flavours of preserved lemons, honey, angelica and lime. Especially lime.

Admittedly, the wines don't often taste like that at the very beginnning. They have a more grassy, lean character, although that lime juice usually makes them succulent and characterful. But after a few years in bottle, Semillon comes over all toasty and rich, as if spread with lime marmalade and honeycomb, yet strangely still dry. It's seriously attractive wine, Semillon, and if you're bored with oaky Chardonnay but still hanker after a full-on flavour, then make it your next stop. Despite its appeal, this is an underrated style of wine, set to become more popular as the craze for Chardonnay wears off. Not all the great Semillons are exclusively made in Australia, by the way – a few worthwhile ones are now being made in South Africa and Argentina, too.

BORDEAUX

Sémillon from Bordeaux can be extraordinarily good: rounded and weighty, with lemony freshness, and again, that honeyed, almost smokey/nutty appeal once aged. It's often blended with the zestier Sauvignon Blanc and aged in oak barrels to add extra depth and flavour. The top white Bordeaux in this style can be a knock-out, but be prepared to shell out for it. Oh, and you'll need a good cellar as they take a long time in bottle to mellow out and reach their best.

As with Chardonnay in Burgundy, they don't put 'Sémillon' on the label in Bordeaux, but many whites from the area contain this grape. Not all, though, will be rich and flavoursome. In fact, a lot of cheap white Bordeaux is dilute and tart. Go for the glorious châteaux of Graves and Pessac-Léognan if you want to taste the most serious and exciting.

Sémillon also makes more humble, everyday whites in the wider south-west region of France, again, usually blended with Sauvignon Blanc. These easy-drinking, zesty-grassy dry wines are not expensive and should be enjoyed while young. Watch out for patchy quality at the basic, inexpensive end of Bordeaux blanc and try to trade up.

SWEETER WINES

An extra word is needed on dessert wines made from Sémillon as these are very important both in and around Bordeaux and in other parts of the New World wine countries. This grape is especially susceptible to botrytis (a mould that is key to the production of sweet wines), as it has a thin skin which is easily attacked by the noble rot. In Bordeaux it is paired with Sauvignon Blanc once more to create some sublime, and very expensive dessert wines – the most famous come from Sauternes and Barsac. In the New World Semillon is used on its own to make rich, peachy sweet wines, especially in Australia. More on dessert wine on pages 148-149.

BLENDS

NOT ALL RICH, OAKY WHITES ARE MADE FROM ONE HUNDRED PERCENT OF ONE GRAPE. Others are a blend of grapes, such as Semillon-Chardonnay blends from Australia. These popular wines are reliable, clean, soft and fruity – a little one-dimensional perhaps, but great value at parties when everyone should enjoy their fruity appeal. Then there's the blend of Roussanne and Marsanne in the Rhône Valley, and the winning combination of Sémillon and leaner, grassier Sauvignon Blanc in Bordeaux. Wine-lovers seem particularly keen on single varieties at the moment, but do try blends as well. They are not necessarily any better, but neither are they any worse.

VIOGNIER

For fans of perfumed, heady, full-bodied white, wines made from the Viognier grape are a must. And for every fashion-conscious wine-lover, Viognier is currently top of the list.

FRANCE

All grapes from the Rhône Valley in France seem to be enjoying a vogue of late, and that's where this exotic white vine comes from. Viognier (pronounced Vee-on-yeh) is seriously cool in wine-drinking circles right now. Which is a good thing when you get your hands on an impressive bottle, and a big disappointment when you come across a dud.

The problem with Viognier, you see, is that if it is made properly, with low-yielding vines, and thus concentrated grapes, and careful work in the winery, it is sublime:

a long lingering mouthful of squashy ripe peaches, dried apricots, with a gorgeous fragrance of honeysuckle and white blossom. No other wine conjures up heady late summer so well.

But, sadly, there are lots of dilute versions around which don't have much perfume, and which are insipid or taste of artificial pear-drops. These have simply been made from vines with high yields of grapes, which may be fine for the grower who wants to sell a lot of fruit, but means that the resulting wine lacks that all-important perfumed peachiness. Sometimes a flabby and disappointing Viognier means it has become too ripe, losing its crispness and concentration. You get the picture – Viognier needs attention in the vineyard and it is not always great, although when you catch the scent of a good one, you'll see what all the fuss is about.

To make sure you get that natural peachy fruit and lovely aroma, pick one from the Condrieu area of the Rhône. These wines are opulent, intense and heady…and extremely expensive. The south of France, especially the Languedoc, makes cheaper, less concentrated versions. These offer a reasonable introduction to Viognier, but avoid bargain-basement ones which can lack acidity and can be disappointingly dull. Viognier is sometimes blended into red wines to add perfume and elegance, particularly in the Rhône. Look out for it added to Syrah there – and recently to a few Shirazes in the New World.

REST OF THE WORLD

Since Viognier became so sought-after, it hasn't been a surprise to see the newer wine-producing countries have a go at it. Most successful is the U.S., where a few decent rich wines with firm, crisp acidity are being produced in California. You might come across one or two fairly well-made Viogniers from Argentina, Australia and South Africa, too. Seek them out. They will be fruit-driven, packed with peaches and held together with a creamy seam of oak. Expect more Viogniers to appear on the scene since this grape is so much in vogue. And of course, because winemakers love a challenge!

Again, beware those which are either too bland or too nail-varnishy in character. Perhaps this is the white version of Pinot Noir – it can be impressive but it can be a disappointment. But it's worth persevering if you like fruity, characterful whites and it's likely more good examples may appear in due course as winemakers perfect their Viognier technique!

OTHER RICH, OAKY WHITES

PLENTY MORE TO PICK FROM

ROUSSANNE AND MARSANNE

The unusual flavours of these wines are increasingly appreciated. They will appeal to anyone who likes their wines forward and full, but is tired of those modern, bright, 'fruit-salad' styles of white.

They may not be very famous (yet), but this duo of grapes is responsible for the superior white wines of the Rhône, like St-Péray, St-Joseph, and Crozes-Hermitage. These wines are not fresh and fruity in the way that Viognier is; they are full-bodied and waxy, weighty, with a deep colour and flavours of nut oil, peach kernel, spice and sometimes aniseed. With age they grow honeyed. Intrigued? Then try these white Rhônes. They go particularly well with savoury food. These are not wines to enjoy on their own as they taste too heavy and lacking in crisp fruit, but match them with fish or chicken in creamy sauces and they come into their own. Not much is made from these grapes around the world, but watch this space. Winemakers in Australia and California in particular are intrigued by the unusual flavours of Rhône whites, and are trying to make their own versions. A few (very oaky) Marsannes are making an appearance and it's only a matter of time before more hit the shelves. You might come across a big, aromatic Marsanne from the south of France in the meantime.

PINOT GRIS

This grape is very rarely oaked, but choose the right label and you can have another full-on, rich white wine. Okay, so Pinot Grigio, as the Italians call it, is anything but rich, and this grape is very rarely oaked. But try the version of Pinot Gris made in Alsace, in eastern France, and bingo! You've got another full-on white wine. The grape is often called Tokay-Pinot Gris here, although it has nothing to do with the sweet wine called Tokay made in Hungary. Here we're talking about a rounded, almost fat white wine, that looks thickly textured in the glass, and is mouth-filling and weighty on the palate. It smells and tastes smoky, spicy, orangey, dry yet ripe, and it is great with rich food such as smooth pâté, confit de canard, roast goose. Not a wishy-washy wine at all, and a million miles away in style from other crisp, light Pinot Gris made around the world (for more on these see pages 28-9).

VIURA/MALVASIA

No chapter on rich whites would be complete without mention of one of the most rich, sultry and heavily oaked dry wines of all time: classic white Rioja. Made in the north of Spain mainly from the local Viura grape, with the help of Malvasia and Garnacho Blanco grapes in the blend, this wine won't please everyone. Deep yellow, waxily thick, reeking of wood and sawdust, and tasting of vanilla and cream, traditional white Rioja rests in barrel for years to take on such a big oak influence. It's a classic, old-fashioned style of wine, nowadays winning fewer fans as people expect brighter, younger, fresh fruit flavours. Do give it a try, though, matched with creamy, savoury dishes or smoked fish, which will stand up to the oaky wine nicely. Sadly, this style of Rioja is being replaced to an extent by younger, leaner, crisper styles. Shame – we need all the styles of wine the world can give us if we are not to sink into uniformity.

MAKING THE DIFFERENCE

SOME OAKY WHITE WINES ARE FERMENTED IN SMALL BARRELS (CALLED BARRIQUES IN FRANCE), AND LEFT TO AGE THERE. Others are simply aged in the barrels after fermentation in tanks. French and American oak are the most commonly used for reds and whites – American oak gives a more overt vanilla flavour than French. A cheaper method of getting some oak flavour into wine is to soak oak chips in a vat of wine. This is perfectly legal (although it gives a cruder flavour than barrels), but the use of laboratory-concocted oak essence is generally not allowed.

STORING AND SERVING

SERVE ALL DRY WHITES, INCLUDING THESE BLOCKBUSTERS, WELL-CHILLED, STRAIGHT FROM THE FRIDGE, AND KEEP THEM COLD WITH AN ICE BUCKET. Splash them into large-bowled glasses – perhaps red wine glasses – filling them only halfway up so you can swirl the liquid easily and savour its heady aroma. All powerful whites should be pleasant to drink on release, and don't necessarily need cellaring. Simple wines like basic Chardonnays, cheap Viogniers and blends of Semillon/Chardonnay need opening quickly after purchase. But the top Chardonnays will mellow out and grow more attractive, soft and integrated with a couple of years' age, and fine burgundies grow wonderfully rounded, inviting and nutty with maturity. Don't miss older Australian Semillon, too – it's quite different from the younger stuff: honeyed, toasty and rich. Store all bottles in a cool, dark place on their sides.

MATCHING RICH, OAKY WHITES WITH FOOD

RICH, DRY WHITES DEMAND FOOD. They are not the best wines to choose as aperitifs because they are too powerful. Instead, pair them with roast poultry, chicken in creamy sauces, and full-flavoured fish and seafood such as salmon, crab and lobster. Oaky Chardonnays are great with smoked salmon as the wood flavours chime in with the smokiness. Peachy Viognier is an impressive partner for creamy, mild curries. If you want to pair white wine with meat (pork, beef in creamy sauces), go for the powerful wines described in this chapter, not light, dry whites.

FIRST TASTE

■ DON'T EXPECT SIMPLE REFRESHMENT HERE. The rich, oaky whites should be packed with flavour, probably laced with toasty oak, and with a lingering finish. Not for the faint-hearted!

■ Don't sip a heavily oaked, powerful white wine on a hot summer's day; it isn't a mere thirst-quencher and will taste too heavy. SAVE RICH, OAKY WHITES FOR MATCHING WITH RICH, SAVOURY DISHES.

■ THE BEST POWERFUL WHITES ARE THOSE WITH FINE BALANCE. They have a fresh, crisp acidity running through them, which lifts all that ripeness and rich oak.

■ You don't have to tolerate oakiness to get a rich white as PLENTY OF THESE WINES ARE MADE WITHOUT OAK-AGEING. Try a Viognier or a mature Semillon that hasn't been oaked, or an unoaked Aussie Chardonnay.

■ But fans of the ultra-oaky styles should TRY TRADITIONAL WHITE RIOJA.

■ If you prefer something crisper overall but enjoy the rich fruitiness of grapes like Chardonnay, PICK A CHARDONNAY FROM A COOLER CLIMATE.

BUYER'S GUIDE

■ THE BEST-VALUE RICH WHITES ARE SOUTHERN FRENCH CHARDONNAYS AND THOSE FROM CHILE. Hungarian ones can be a bargain, and South Africa offers more serious stuff at a decent price. Don't buy the cheapest white burgundy as it is patchy in quality, and tread carefully among the lower-priced Californians.

■ Top burgundies, Viogniers from the Rhône, and the best labels from Australia and California are as good as it gets in this style category. DO TRY TO SPLASH OUT on them now and again to see what the very best can be like.

■ DON'T GIVE IN TO FASHION. If you love the older styles of very oaky Aussie Chardonnay, then fine. Or if you dislike ultra-trendy Viognier, don't drink it! The rich, oaky whites have always swung in and out of fashion more than other types of wine as they are such distinctive styles. Stick to what you like – regardless of trends!

■ KNOW YOUR OAK, whether it's to avoid it or to search out oaky whites. Look for words such as barrel-fermented or *barrique/chêne* (France) or *crianza* (Spain) on a label to indicate ageing in oak casks. Some lighter Chardonnays might state that they are unoaked or lightly oaked, which all helps you choose a style you like.

MOVING ON

■ DON'T JUST STICK TO CHARDONNAY. Not all the best rich whites are made from this one famous grape variety. Try some of the other grapes recommended in this section; that way you won't get bored with just one set of flavours. What about Sémillon, Viognier or Marsanne?

■ And if you do buy a lot of Chardonnay, be sure to try out lots of different bottles. NOT ALL CHARDONNAY TASTES THE SAME, by any means. Go for a new region, a new producer, an older wine or one with a less oaky character. Don't get stuck in a rut! Other Chardonnay styles are discussed in the section on 'Sparkling Wines' (see pages 106–141).

■ TRY BLENDS OF GRAPES, TOO – Chardonnay with Sémillon, or Roussanne with Marsanne. Don't just stick to single-varietal wines.

■ The rich, oaky whites can get tiresome – too loud and overpowering. MAKE SURE YOU BUY RELATIVELY FRESH AND WELL-BALANCED WINES, match them with the correct food, and regularly ring the changes with other types of wine. Investigate them thoroughly, and if you are getting bored, treat yourself to a top burgundy or southern-hemisphere Chardonnay, or a Condrieu, to remind yourself how fabulous rich, oaky whites can be!

SPARKLING WINE PUTS MORE CONSUMERS IN A DITHER THAN ANY OTHER STYLE. What is Champagne, exactly? Will a cheap fizz do just as well? Do I always have to spend a fortune on a famous label? How do I open the bottle, let alone store and serve it? Does it go with food? Wine with bubbles costs a lot more than wine without (I'll explain why later on), so it is understandable that we want to know exactly how best to spend our precious pennies.

The pressure to get it right is only exacerbated by the fact that fizz is usually brought out on special occasions. Ironically, this means we often fail to notice its shortcomings. People might sweat over which bubbly to serve at their darling daughter's wedding, but on the big day itself, everyone is far too busy chattering, listening to speeches and dancing to notice a painfully thin and acidic wine in their glass – unpleasant traits they may have spotted had they cracked open a bottle one quiet Tuesday night. Still, think hard, and I'm sure you will remember a moment when an expensive fizz has disappointed. There are plenty of hints on the following pages to help you avoid a repeat performance and instead make Champagne and sparkling wines enhance life's joyful moments.

Certainly, there is nothing else in the wine world to touch Champagne for glamour and kudos. The packaging is often ornate and classy, the brands glittering and famous, the price tag scarily high. It all adds to the impression that you are buying a touch of luxury. But I wish we took sparkling wine less seriously in the UK. Go to Australia and they crack open a bottle of inexpensive, locally produced bubbly on an everyday basis, yet still drink Champagne on a momentous occasion. Fizzy wine comes in so many different styles and at so many different price points that we deserve to ring the changes more often. Let your life sparkle a little more!

TEXTURE

Champagne can be pretty rich and complex, but the high acidity and fine streams of tiny bubbles give a light impression and provide a refreshing lift to the wine.

APPEARANCE

Most sparklers are pale and straw-coloured, although pink fizz ranges from a delicate onion-skin hue to a rich, sunset crimson. The look of the bubbles is important, too: they should be tiny, rather than large and coarse, and there should be plenty of them.

AROMA

There's a fresh, fruity perfume, often lemons, sometimes more orangey or appley, perhaps with hints of peaches and raspberries (especially in rosé). A lot of fizz has a distinct yeastiness, too, which sometimes comes across as fresh bread, brioche or even Marmite! Look out for creamy, yoghurty aromas, as well as biscuit in some sparklers and milk chocolate in others.

FLAVOUR

Crisp, tangy acidity is a must in a good sparkler to give a refreshing, mouth-watering finish. As with the aromas, that fresh, clean fruit should be there, and the same hints of yeast, yoghurt and chocolate, particularly on the finish. Champagne is sometimes described as having a 'double' taste: a clean, incisively crisp attack followed by richer, creamier depths after swallowing.

CHAMPAGNE

THE MOST GORGEOUS
SPARKLER IN THE WORLD

First things first. Champagne is only really Champagne when it comes from the Champagne region of northeast France. Any other bubbly is sparkling wine and so must not use the 'Ch...' word on its label.

At the top end of the quality ladder, the best Champagne is still the most gorgeous sparkler in the world. Why is it so special? Firstly, the Champenois have been making sparkling wine for centuries – ever since monks there discovered how to create bubbles, probably by mistake in the seventeenth century – so they have a high level of expertise. Rules and regulations exist to ensure a certain level of quality (though there have been good and bad times for general quality). Most important are the natural conditions in this part of France – the chalky soils and the cool climate – that help to create a thin, acidic base wine. When put through a second fermentation with the resulting bubbles trapped in the liquid, and aged in the bottle, this creates a sparkling wine of finesse and complexity.

The best Champagnes combine a certain amount of power – plenty of rich fruit, layers of rich cream, yeast, bread and chocolate – with remarkable elegance: a fine and enchanting balance. They are among the most effective appetite-whetters in the world, with mouth-watering crispness and palate-teasing bubbles, and yet they also go well with fish, seafood and even light chicken and vegetarian dishes. Some Champagnes are at their most delightful when they are young and vivacious, while others age well, mellowing gracefully into more honeyed, toffeed wines with a mere prickle of gas on the tongue. No wonder Champagne is still so revered and adored around the world. Most other sparklers just seem unsubtle and a little clumsy by comparison.

That said – and you probably knew this was coming – there are plenty of poor Champagnes that let the side down, though fewer than there used to be. The main problems are a sour acidity, high enough to create an involuntary wince, and what has been described as a 'lean, mean, green' character. In other words, a lack of ripeness and a reliance on very young wine in the blend, rather than extra-aged reserve blending wine. In the late eighties and early nineties, these cheap and nasty Champagnes seemed to proliferate. After protests from critics and consumers, the Champenois successfully raised the general quality.

To avoid the tooth-rotting nasties that still lurk out there, give the very cheapest Champagnes a miss (switch to other types of sparkling wine at reasonable prices), but pick a reliable name and never drink vintage Champagne when it is too young. Although non-vintage – a blend from different years – is meant to be consumed soon after release, vintage should be kept for several years after purchase or it can taste raw and tart.

The meticulous, time-consuming technique for producing Champagne is called the *méthode traditionnelle*, also known as *méthode champenoise*, and is used throughout the region. The basic wine is put into heavy bottles, which must be thick or they would crack under the pressure of the gassy wine, then a little yeast and sugar solution is introduced and the bottle sealed with a metal cap. The wine then re-ferments, trapping the carbon dioxide gas produced in the liquid, and the sediment of dead yeast, also known as the lees, settles. The wine is left to age on its lees, which gives it some yeasty character and richness. The bottles are turned regularly on a rack and twisted at an ever-sharper angle, gradually moving to an upside-down position, with the sediment resting in the neck of the bottle. At the end of this process, the neck is frozen and the bottle opened to release the solid plug of frozen sediment. It is then topped up with a little *dosage*, or sweetened wine, the amount and contents of which help determine the style of the finished wine. Finally the bottle is re-sealed, but this time with the distinctive Champagne cork and wire cage. *Et voilà!*

This careful, slow process has been adopted for fine sparkling wines all over the world. Likewise, the same classic Champagne blend of grapes is sometimes used: Chardonnay, Pinot Noir and Pinot Meunier are the only three grapes allowed in Champagne. The first two are the most important and appear either together in a blend or occasionally as single-varietal wines. A bottle that is labelled *blanc de blancs* Champagne is made from one hundred percent Chardonnay whereas one labelled *blanc de noirs* (literally, white from black) is one

hundred percent Pinot grapes (Noir and Meunier). *Blanc de blancs* tends to be creamier with yellow-fruit flavours, *blanc de noirs* has a red-berry, particularly raspberry, character and is firmer and more aromatic. No one style is necessarily better than another, so go for the wine you like best.

The famous Champagne houses do not necessarily offer the best value for money, considering the prohibitively high prices fetched by many of them. Supermarket own-label Champagnes are very reasonable and have improved enormously over the past decade; in fact, many are now sourced from highly reputable Champagne producers. But sometimes we all prefer to shell out more money for a glamorous label. Among the best of the swanky labels to go for – the ones consistently providing the most delectable wines as well as stylish packaging – are Moët et Chandon,

Veuve Clicquot, Bollinger, Louis Roederer, Ruinart, Krug, Billecart-Salmon, Charles Heidsieck, Lanson, Pol Roger and Taittinger. Less well-known but impressive Champagne houses include Jacquesson, Joseph Perrier, the cooperative Jacquart and Gosset. Also, look out for wines made by the grape-growers themselves as these often offer terrific value for money. Good 'grower' Champagnes include Gimonnet and Goutorbe.

The vast majority of bottles sold are *brut* (dry), but do give other styles of Champagne a whirl. To enjoy them at their best, try each at the right moment. *Demi-sec* (sweeter with honeyed overtones) is lovely served with fruit puddings or cakes – it's certainly better with wedding cake than *brut*. *Sec* is in between the previous two styles, so serve it with somewhat sweet-tasting savoury canapés, perhaps pâté or seafood. Rosé can be a delight, usually made by adding small amounts of red Pinot Noir wine from the Bouzy or Aÿ areas of Champagne to the blend. It is fruitier, tasting overtly of red berries and peaches, and goes well with prawns, salmon and lobster. And, of course, it's the ultimate in romantic drinks.

Serve all Champagnes well-chilled and drink up soon after opening; otherwise they will go flat quickly. There are various methods for keeping Champagne fizzy overnight, but, in my view, nothing quite tastes the same as a freshly opened, fabulously fizzy bottle.

CRÉMANT

For Francophiles who don't want to splash out on Champagne, or if you want cheaper fizz to drink everyday, *crémant* is the next best thing. This category of French fizz, created in the 1980s, aims to provide regulated, good-quality bubbly made in the *méthode traditionnelle*, but from other parts of France.

As with Champagne, there are rules and regulations that apply to *crémant* production and, although different grape varieties are permitted in different areas, in very general terms, the results are pretty impressive considering the relatively low prices charged. Crémant d'Alsace is clean, tangy and fresh, rather leaner and more mineral in style than Champagne. Crémant de Bourgogne tends to be made from Chardonnay and Pinot Noir – the same grapes as Champagne – and is aromatic with fruity, red-berry flavours. Crémant de Loire is lemony, zingy and has a crisp mousse. Crémant de Limoux is refreshing, creamy... And so on. Many people discover a local crémant while on holiday in France, so if you stumble across one at home or abroad, then do give it a go.

REST OF FRANCE

Sadly, there is an ocean of cheap and very nasty fizz made in France. That bargain bottle with a plastic stopper, bought in Calais with some spare change, may well turn out to be sickly sweet and artificial tasting or, even worse, metallic or rubbery in character. Buyer beware! My strong advice to those stocking up for a special occasion is always, but *always*, try one bottle of cheap fizz before committing to a boot-load. And do sample a wine called Clairette de Die Tradition or Clairette de Die Méthode Dioise Ancestrale, if you see it. Produced around the town of Die on the River Drôme, a tributary of the Rhône, these are gently frothy, grapily refreshing, off-dry sparklers made partly with the perfumed Muscat grape. They are great with cakes and fruit.

CAVA

A TREAT FOR SPARKLING-WINE LOVERS

One of the most common misconceptions surrounding fizz is that cava is a type of sparkling wine made around the world. It is, in fact, a purely Spanish wine. Like sherry and Rioja, cava is one of this country's great classics. Cava is fresh, dry and fairly neutral, with appley notes and sometimes a mineral quality. It may not be especially exciting, but as such it is refreshing, reliable and remarkably well-priced.

Cava is produced mainly in the region of Penedés, on the eastern edge of Spain, and is made in the same laborious way as Champagne, which is quite astonishing when you consider the price difference between the two. Cava is not made from the same grapes as Champagne, though. Instead, a trio of local Spanish grapes is used – Macabeo, Parellada and Xarel-lo – although some quality-conscious (and fashion-conscious) producers include Chardonnay in the blend to add a modern, rounded and fruity note. Wines are made and aged in the huge cellars that lie under the town of San Sadurni de Noya.

Vintage cava from one fine year is a treat for sparkling-wine lovers. The best examples, from a top producer like Juvé y Camps, taste richer and more rounded but with that same sprightly apple character at the core, and not a bit like Champagne. The enormous popularity of cava is still growing, despite the threat from non-European bubblies. Cava now accounts for nearly fifty percent of the sparkling-wine market in the UK. That's an awful lot of bubbles. As long as prices stay low, and the cheapest supermarket own-label bottles remain so reliable, we shall continue to adore this wine.

PROSECCO

ITALY'S MOST MOREISH FIZZ

Prosecco is Italy's most moreish fizz, made from the grape variety of the same name around the hills of Treviso in Veneto, to the northeast. The best wines are labelled 'Superiore di Cartizze'. Look for the word frizzante on the label as this means a style with a gentler mousse – more froth than fizz.

ASTI

Asti is perhaps a more famous Italian sparkling wine. Snobs are often patronising about this sweet, grapey wine – not officially called Spumante anymore, but now simply Asti – but its many fans find it sadly underrated. Certainly, a fresh, youthful Asti served frostily cold with desserts, cakes, sweet biscuits or on its own at the end of a rich feast is wonderfully uplifting and palate-cleansing. Its naturally low alcohol is a bonus, too, after lots of other, more heady wines. All too often, however, it is served at room temperature as an aperitif when a dry fizz would be so much more appealing. Save Asti's reputation, and drink it at the right moment.

If you still think it sounds naff, try its superior cousin Moscato d'Asti, which is a little less sweet with a softer, spritzier mousse. It is slightly higher in alcohol and costs a little more, but is generally more delicious and is taken a bit more seriously by wine buffs. Look out for the words *Valdobbiadene* or *Conegliano* on the label as these small areas produce the highest quality Proseccos.

OTHER SPARKLERS

PLENTY MORE TO PICK FROM

GERMANY AND AUSTRIA

Germany and Austria both make sparkling wines labelled Sekt, usually from Riesling, Pinot Blanc and Welschriesling varieties. Watch out for cheap and nasty German examples that are often sulphurous; think burnt rubber or struck matches – very unpleasant. Occasionally a tasty example comes along, and any visitor to Vienna may well enjoy a glass of cold Sekt in a bar. There's something about Sekt that makes it nicer in situ than at home, and anyway, its fragile nature means it doesn't travel well. The best you can expect, however, is a zesty, dry, bubbly mouthful. The Austrian producer Bründlmayer makes the finest Sekt I have come across.

ENGLAND

Recently, England has become the unlikely source of some rather exciting sparkling wines made in the traditional method (see the 'Champagne' section on page 114-118). Or is it so unlikely? England's cool climate, which is not so very different from that of the Champagne region in northern France, and the chalky soils in parts of the south make it ideal for producing a simple, tart, base wine for fizz. English winemakers are rapidly developing their skills for sparklers and the result is a bumper crop of quality bubblies, some of which have won awards in international competitions for their poise and elegance. Let's hear it for Nyetimber, Camel, Ridgeview and Valley Vineyards, among others, championing English sparklers effectively for the first time.

THE NEW WORLD

There are now some super sparklers from newer parts of the winemaking globe: New Zealand, Australia, California and so on. There are three interesting facts to note here. One, the *méthode traditionnelle* is widely employed to create the best examples, as are the two most important grape varieties used in Champagne – Chardonnay and Pinot Noir.

Secondly, Champagne houses are heavily involved in the production of much of the finest overseas fizz. Louis Roederer's Californian offshoot, which makes a wine called Quartet; Deutz Marlborough Cuvée in New Zealand; and Moët et Chandon's Green Point from Australia, are all cases in point. Even Cloudy Bay's classy, rich sparkler, Pelorus, has had some input from Veuve Clicquot. Clearly the Champenois know a good opportunity when they see one and believe there is a healthy market out there for both Champagne and sparkling wine.

Thirdly, southern-hemisphere winemakers have only become successful at fizz since they started sourcing grapes from cool-climate vineyards. Hot spots simply don't make fizz with finesse.

AUSTRALIA

Take Australian bubbly, for example. There are lots of ripe, sunny, big-bubbled Aussie sparklers, made mainly by cheaper modes of production than the Champagne method. For refined, well-balanced sparkling wine from this country you need grapes – Chardonnay and Pinot Noir, naturally – grown in cool areas such as Tasmania, the Yarra Valley in Victoria and the Adelaide Hills in South Australia.

Some of the cheap-and-cheerful bubblies made by the less expensive methods are actually fine for everyday glugging; Yalumba's Angas Brut has always been reliably fun and fruity. Also, don't miss the chance to try Sparkling Shiraz, purple froth with soft, curranty fruit. Served cold with a barbecue or even on Christmas Day, it can be a jolly and unusual way to drink bubbly. Okay, we know it's not white…

NEW ZEALAND

New Zealand is an exciting place for fizz. The Marlborough region on the South Island has the right conditions – a long, cool ripening season – suitable for Chardonnay and Pinot base wine. It provides some good-value labels with pure, bright fruit flavours and crisp acidity – in fact, typical of the region's still wines.

SOUTH AFRICA

South Africa makes sparklers by the traditional Champagne method, which it calls *Méthode Cap Classique*, or MCC. Despite the fact that some of the packaging is old-fashioned and garish, Cape sparklers can be surprisingly good, even from warmer spots. Graham Beck leads the way with his range from the hot spot of Robertson, and winemakers from the pretty valley of Franschhoek have come up with impressively fresh and snappy wines in the past. Some inexpensive, non-MCC Cape fizz has been successful in export markets.

These are made mainly by cheaper methods of production and from grapes other than Chardonnay and Pinot Noir. Brands such as Kumala and Arniston Bay may be popular, but lack finesse and character. Stick to MCC wines if you can trade up.

US

California is home to some highly successful producers of refined sparkling wine, made by the Champagne method and from the Champagne grapes. The cooler spots, such as Anderson Valley and Carneros, turn out superb grapes for fizz. Some of these wines are very classy indeed.

There aren't many decent sparklers made in South America that I can recommend. You may just pick up a decent fizz from Canada, New York State's Finger Lakes or Oregon, but you are more likely to come across these wines when visiting the area, rather than in your local supermarket.

MAKING THE DIFFERENCE

THE MÉTHODE TRADITIONNELLE, OR CHAMPAGNE METHOD, IS DESCRIBED ON PAGE 116. Other less laborious and cheaper ways to produce fizz include the transfer method, with second fermentation in the bottle, followed by disgorgement into large tanks to remove the sediment, then the addition of sugar solution and rebottling. There is also the tank method, with second fermentation in large pressure tanks to which sugar and yeast have been added, and perhaps even the crudest method of all, pumping carbon dioxide into the liquid to create bubbles. These methods don't produce such good quality fizz and in the case of the last method, they can make fairly unpleasant stuff!

MATCHING SPARKLING WINES WITH FOOD

MOST OF US CAN'T WAIT TO CRACK OPEN A BOTTLE OF FIZZ AND DRINK IT ON ITS OWN AS A TOAST, A CELEBRATION OR A SEDUCTION TOOL! But hold on a second. Although brut, with its crisp acidity and refreshing bubbles, is a great aperitif, it is also a good partner for light canapés, seafood, fish dishes and, in the case of the richest wines, even light chicken recipes. Try sweeter styles of sparkling wine with fresh fruit and light desserts. Dry rosé makes a good partner for seafood, especially prawns.

STORING AND SERVING

AS A RULE OF THUMB, CHEAP FIZZ NEEDS DRINKING UP QUICKLY OR IT WILL LOSE ITS FRESH APPEAL. Open non-vintage cava, most non-European sparklers and most non-vintage Champagne within a few weeks of purchase. The poshest non-vintage Champagne will last longer, say, up to eighteen months, as will the finest vintage cava and superior non-European sparkling wine. Top vintage Champagne, as well as one or two of California's finest, is meant to be cellared, or stashed in any cool, dark place, for several years. It will emerge a more well-knit, mellow wine with less harsh acidity and a slightly richer, honeyed quality. Well worth the wait, in other words.

SERVING SPARKLERS

The age-old problem of how to open sparkling wine seems to defeat many, including Formula One drivers. There is a technique to this, however, and once mastered, you will be amazed how simple it seems. This is why waiters almost always impress when they open a bottle of fizz; it looks as though there is a secret to it, but they are simply following a few guidelines.

Of course, shaking the bottle vigorously and popping it open suddenly is the worst thing to do, especially if it's a Champagne that cost a fortune! Bubbly is under enormous pressure, so if you don't open it slowly and carefully, the cork could explode from the bottle, wasting your fizz, and possibly putting someone's eye out. I'm not joking – opening sparkling wine and Champagne can be dangerous – so

make sure the bottle isn't pointing at anyone. It's best to aim up at the point where wall meets ceiling. Hold the bottle at an angle as it is less likely to fizz up and out in a rush. It's also worth knowing that well-chilled fizz is less explosive.

The best way to open your bubbly is to hold the base of the bottle firmly in one hand (use a dry tea-towel to grip it if damp), and with the other hand, undo the foil wrap and the wire cage. As you take the wire cage off, keep a couple of fingers hovering over the cork, prepared to contain an explosion at any point. Then gently, slowly, twist the bottle one way, and the cork the other, aiming to prise it out gradually. The result is a soft, satisfying hiss as the cork is released into your hand, and very little fizz, if any at all, should be lost.

CHAMPAGNE GLASSES

SERVE IN TALL, ELEGANT FLUTES, PREFERABLY WITH PLAIN BOWLS SO THAT YOU CAN SEE THE PRETTY COLOUR OF THE WINE AND THE TINY STREAMS OF BUBBLES RISING THROUGH THE LIQUID. Fill right up (flutes don't suit being half full, and anyway, it's hard to swirl fizz) and pour gently, holding the glass at an angle so the liquid doesn't froth too much and overflow.

The traditional wide, shallow-bowled Champagne glasses (said to have been made in honour of Marie-Antoinette's breasts) look luxurious, but have fallen out of fashion in favour of tall flutes. This is partly because the bubbles in sparkling wine dissipate more quickly in wide bowls as there is simply more surface area for them to pop up to. Flat fizz isn't the idea at all, so many people now prefer flutes, which seem to retain the sparkle more effectively.

Hold the base of the bottle firmly in one hand, and with the other hand, undo the foil wrap and wire cage.

Gently, slowly, twist the bottle one way, and the cork the other, aiming to prise it out gradually.

FIRST TASTE

■ LOOK OUT FOR DIFFERENT LEVELS OF
RICHNESS. Some sparklers are distinctly lean and green
with unappetisingly high acidity. Better bottles have a
riper, creamier quality, more layers of flavour and a
lingering finish. Avoid the high-acid monsters!

■ Try sweeter styles of sparkling wine – *demi-sec* or even
the slightly less dry *sec*. *Brut* accounts for most of the fizz
sold, but THERE ARE SOME OCCASIONS WHEN
SWEETER SPARKLERS ARE MORE APPROPRIATE.
Fizz comes in unusual styles, too – not just *brut*, white
and French! Try an English sparkler, a sweet, frothy
Moscato d'Asti, or a red sparkling Shiraz from Australia.

■ If you ever get the chance, SAMPLE MATURE
VINTAGE CHAMPAGNE. Most is consumed too young,
so tasting one that is ten years or more in age can be a
revelation – a quite different experience to endless bottles
of youthful fizz. Look for rich, honeyed, toasty nuances.

■ AVOID ULTRA-CHEAP FRENCH FIZZ, as it is often
disappointing. For better quality, go for Champagne or
French *crémant*. Always, always SERVE SPARKLING
WINE AND CHAMPAGNE CHILLED and soon after
opening the bottle. Old, warm fizz is plain horrible!

BUYER'S GUIDE

■ Avoid cheap, discounted Champagne from unknown labels. It may well be thin and over-acidic. Instead, GO FOR A NON-EUROPEAN SPARKLING WINE OR CAVA FOR INEXPENSIVE EVERYDAY BUBBLES.

■ SOME SUPERMARKET OWN-LABEL CHAMPAGNES ARE GOOD VALUE FOR MONEY. Try one bottle before committing to a wedding-load, though.

■ CAVA IS ONE OF THE BEST PARTY WINES THERE IS. It is almost always fresh, dry, crisp and neutral. Serve on its own, mixed with orange juice for Buck's Fizz or with crème de cassis for pretend Kir Royales.

■ CRÉMANT IS A GOOD-VALUE ALTERNATIVE TO CHAMPAGNE. Quality varies a bit, but you should find something palatable for a good price.

■ NEW ZEALAND ALSO OFFERS EXCELLENT SPARKLERS, which are fruity and lively in style, probably the best of all in the mid-price bracket.

■ Californian sparkling wine can be fabulous, but it will cost a lot. SPLASH OUT ON A TOP WEST COAST WINE for a special occasion as an alternative to fine Champagne.

MOVING ON

■ Once you are familiar with the distinctive characteristics of Champagne, TRY WINES FROM DIFFERENT HOUSES, not just the well-known ones. Sample some less famous names and the growers and producers who grow their own grapes. Some are mentioned in this chapter.

■ AGE SOME DECENT VINTAGE CHAMPAGNE. Some people like very mature Champagne, others prefer it more youthful and sprightly. Find out which suits you best. If you can afford it, stash away a few bottles and open one each New Year to see when it reaches the optimum stage of development for you.

■ Don't just drink it on its own, TRY MATCHING CHAMPAGNE WITH FOOD. Simple light canapés, fish and chicken are all easy matches. Try caviar, sushi and mildly spicy Asian dishes with fizz, too.

■ TEST OUT THE BEST NAMES FROM AUSTRALIA, CALIFORNIA AND EVEN ENGLAND, places where they are now capable of making serious sparkling wine. Does it match up to Champagne, in your view?

A SPECIAL OCCASION

THOSE ORGANISING A WEDDING OR OTHER SPECIAL OCCASION TEND TO FALL PREY TO ACUTE 'WINE WORRY'. After all, the day will be ruined if the wines aren't perfect, won't it? Well, no, actually – most people are too busy chatting and dancing to care much about what's in their glass. Fussy old Uncle Henry is far more likely to notice a poor wine when he is relaxing at home on his own or dining out, and actually giving some serious thought to his food and drink. But it is understandable that wedding planners, or anyone organising a special event, want everything to be spot-on – especially if a lot of money is being spent on the booze. On the following pages are some tips to help out those with the jitters.

CHOOSING SPECIAL WINES

▓ You do not need to buy expensive Champagne for a
big event – in fact, you don't have to have Champagne at
all! If you do decide to splash out, go for a reliable big
name or a cheaper Champers that you have tasted in
advance. BEWARE PRICEY VINTAGE CHAMPAGNES
THAT ARE NOT MATURE (they should be at least six
years old). And plenty of non-European sparklers, French
crémants and Spanish cavas will go down just as well as
inferior Champagnes – often for a fraction of the price.

▓ One idea is to buy a few bottles of fine Champagne
for the toasts, and lots of cheaper fizz for the rest of the
bash. CONSIDER MAGNUMS AS WELL.

▓ Make sure your fizz is brut (dry) – THIS IS NOT THE
MOMENT FOR SWEET SPARKLING WINE like Asti,
unless it is specifically to serve with a celebration cake.

▓ Don't be tempted by a seriously cut-price, unknown
wine from a discount warehouse (unless you get a good
taste of it first), it could well be a dud. TRADE UP FROM
THE BARGAIN BASEMENT, sticking to medium price
brackets for something safe and palatable.

■ Make sure the wines are relatively young and fresh, and BE SURE TO HAVE CHILLED THE WHITES AND SPARKLERS. Ensure even the reds are not too jammily hot. Warm wine will taste horrible, especially in an over-crowded, over-heated event.

■ If booking a venue where you are required to serve house wines, BE SURE TO TASTE THEM WELL IN ADVANCE OF YOUR EVENT. If they are poor, say so and ask for something different.

■ CHOOSE EASY-DRINKING, SOFT, FRUITY STYLES OF WINE – not ones with 'difficult' characteristics. Aim to buy crowd-pleasers that slip down easily, and don't be tempted to show off with unusual styles.

■ TRUST YOUR INSTINCTS. Get in a few different bottles for a mini-tasting and pick one or two of your favourites. Good luck!

SWEET WINES

No book on white wines is complete without a word on sweet wines. Although the majority of white wines are dry or off-dry, most people enjoy a glass of luscious, sticky pudding wine at the end of a meal. These are often made from the same grape varieties as their favourite dry wines!

There are some divine sweet wines out there, but unfortunately some sickly, cloying ones too. A good dessert wine not only has plenty of sugar, but fresh acidity to balance it out and give the wine a clean refreshing 'lift'. When you get a good one – a decent Sauternes, or fine Austrian Beerenauslese for example – you can see what the fuss is all about. There's something about the pairing of a wonderful dessert with a small, frosted glass of perfectly chilled sweet wine that is quite sublime. So what are good dessert wines like?

TEXTURE Should be richer and thicker than dry whites. Expect a honeyed texture, almost viscous. In some very rich, mature examples, the texture can be quite treacley.

APPEARANCE The majority of dessert wines, including those from Bordeaux, the Loire, Germany and Austria, are a deep, bright-gold. A few sticky pudding wines are ruddy-red or mahogany brown.

AROMA Some have floral scents; jasmine is typical of Muscat. The aroma is fruity; apricot and peach, lemon and orange are common. You may notice toffee or nutty notes, too.

FLAVOUR More apricot, plenty of honey, beeswax, barley sugar, preserved lemons and quinces, with a crisp clean finish. That's in the good ones, anyway!

From France: Semillon/Sauvignon blends, such as Sauternes and Barsac, are enticing, but expensive. A cheaper, simpler version is Monbazillac. Sweet Loire wines made from Chenin Blanc and fortified Muscats from the south are more affordable. Alsace produces sweet, late-harvest versions of its spicy whites, mainly from Pinot Gris, Gewurztraminer and Riesling.

Talking of Riesling, sweet German whites can have great finesse and a fresh, clean character. Try Rieslings labelled Beerenauslese and Trocken-beerenauslese or Eiswein (made from frozen grapes) for the best pudding styles. Austria also makes superb dessert wines, especially from the Neusiedlersee region of Burgenland. Again, some of the top bottles are made from Riesling.

Italy produces, among others, the divine Vin Santo – from the syrup of shrivelled grapes that have been left to dry before being squeezed. Spain offers good-value Moscatel de Valencia, and Hungary the majestic, irresistable Tokaji, made from a paste of nobly rotten grape (see below) added to a fermented base wine. It tastes of marmalade and caramel.

Certain New World countries make excellent sweet wines. Sip Australia's fruity, botrytised Semillons, New Zealand's pure-tasting Rieslings and Canada's amazingly concentrated yet clean, crisp Icewine, made from the elixir produced from frozen grapes!

Botrytis (noble) rot is key to many top sweet wines. In certain natural conditions, the mould *Botrytis cinerea* attacks ripe grapes on the vine in the autumn. Unlike any other mould, botrytis reduces the grape's water content, concentrating the sugar, preserving the acidity and adding unusual characteristics – a waxy, slightly decayed apricot and honey flavour, with hints of fresh mushroom and rotting leaves – only much nicer!

PACKAGING WINE

The vast majority of wines sold come in 75cl glass bottles. This standard size of bottle is supposed to be perfect for sharing between two, and anyway, if you don't finish it in one sitting, the wine should keep well for a couple of days. That said, I think there are alternatives that could be considered from time to time.

Half-bottles are a grand idea if you only want a glass or two; I would recommend buying these rather than resealing a bigger bottle as wine does start to deteriorate from the moment it is exposed to air. Pick half-bottles if you are trying out new styles of wine, too, that way it won't matter so much if you choose something you don't like. Always buy halves for the wines that tend to be enjoyed at just one particular time of year, but are rejected the rest of the time. Make more of these small bottles.

Sadly, big bottles are equally overlooked. Why don't we buy more magnums (one and a half litres, the equivalent of two ordinary bottles) or even Jereboams (six bottles)? Larger bottles look great at special celebrations, somehow convincing guests that we have been wildly generous when, in fact, an equal volume of wine bought in ordinary bottles usually costs about the same. Magnums are widely available for premium wine as well as for the cheapies like Lambrusco and Liebfraumilch, although an independent wine merchant may be your best bet for tracking down a wide range of serious big bottles. Jereboams are rarer, and the huge Methuselahs (or eight bottles), Balthazars (sixteen bottles) and Nebuchadnezzars (twenty bottles) are even scarcer, and mainly restricted to Champagne.

If you want to buy large-format bottles for laying down in a cellar, bear in mind that the wine tends to age more slowly in them (and conversely more quickly in halves) – it's to do with the proportion of wine exposed to the sides and top of the bottle. Oh, and they won't fit in your usual wine racks, either!

Bottled wine is sealed with a natural cork, a plastic stopper or a screw cap. An unacceptably high number of bottles is spoilt by the pesky mould that can occur when bark is used to plug a bottle. Metal screw caps are slowly coming into vogue and are being used by more quality wine producers than ever before. Although they seem less classy than natural cork, they fulfil their role of sealing wine well and bring no taint into the equation. Plastic stoppers have similar benefits. Plastic and metal screw caps are, however, not biodegradable and there is some debate over whether they allow wine to age well as they let no air in at all. Despite this, until manufacturers of corks sort out their problems, it's my guess wine drinkers will increasingly seek out these alternative 'closures'. After all, you wouldn't buy milk in cartons if one in every twenty pints was spoilt by its packaging, would you? So why put up with cork taint?

Finally, wine boxes are a convenient container for wine if you are having a party and don't feel like opening bottles all night. Generally, they hold three litres of wine. Don't expect serious, sophisticated wine to come in boxes, as more everyday, easy-drinking styles tend to be packaged in this way. I don't recommend boxes if you plan to siphon off just one glass from time to time, as the wine will deteriorate gradually in this type of packaging – or quickly, if a hole or leak develops in the bag. Use when entertaining crowds, and bear in mind some people think they are a bit naff!

READING THE LABELS

It may be hard to imagine now, but just a few years ago the arrival of straightforward, clear wine labels was a revelation. Let's be honest, a lot of traditional wine labels are difficult to understand, referring as they do to obscure place-names, vineyard sites and different types of producers, such as *domaines*, *châteaux* and *négociants*. Highly parochial references to styles of wine – for example, *Spätlese* for a riper, and *Trocken* for a drier style of German white – make it even trickier to understand what is in the bottle. Thank goodness, then, for the younger winemaking countries which have pioneered labels giving exactly the information ordinary people want to know. The wine is called, let's say, Muddy Creek, the grape is Chardonnay, the year was 2003 and the area was the Hunter Valley, Australia. Hallelujah!

CLASSIC FRENCH LABEL

Grape varieties are not mentioned on traditional Bordeaux labels. Instead the name of the château takes precedence. It's the same in other French regions.

TRADITIONAL GERMAN LABEL

In Germany, the grape variety does appear on the label. Gothic script is common too; it looks old-fashioned, but don't let it put you off these often-great whites.

MODERN, GRAPHIC LABELS

A typical label from a newer wine-producing country is simpler and easier to read. There is less clutter on the label – just a few words telling you the brand, the grape, the vintage and the region. And that's it. Easy!

STYLES OF WINE LABELS

Newer wine-producing countries, such as Australia and Chile, tend towards the same sort of labels: simple and obvious. But the lines are now blurred. Some European producers have followed suit and are turning out highly modern, graphic designs. The south of France and Germany are two places where a lot of modern-style labels are now being produced, mainly for cheapish wines that appeal to the everyday drinker.

As a general rule of thumb, though, the great classic wines of the world, such as Bordeaux, burgundy and German Rieslings, are still packaged under somewhat arcane labels that wine buffs understand, but everyone else tends to find a bit mystifying. I'm not suggesting that all wine should be labelled like an Aussie Chardonnay – we would lose the charming and culturally important traditional terminology of wine.

I'm just pointing out that it isn't easy for beginners to understand wine labels. This is one reason Europe has lost ground to the newer wine-producing regions in recent years.

ELEMENTS TO LOOK OUT FOR

• French wines are often labelled by place rather than the grape variety. You are meant to know the classic grapes of each region.

• Alsace is an exception to this general rule. Winemakers in this region of eastern France do put grape varieties on their labels. Otherwise Alsatian labels can be hard to get to grips with; they look German, sometimes with Germanic names and grapes, such as Riesling, and they even use Gothic script on the label. Be aware, though, that tall, green bottles are not always from Germany; they may come from Alsace, or indeed from Austria or elsewhere.

• The south of France has recently adopted a simpler and more modern approach to labelling, imitating the newer wine regions and naming grape varieties. The wines often taste rather 'New World' in style, too: ripe, fruit-driven and very modern.

• Italian wines are generally not labelled by grape variety either – or rather, the great classics of Tuscany and Piedmont aren't. Modern producers working in the deep south and some of those in the northeast favour grapes appearing on labels.

• In Spain, the term 'oak-ageing' is particularly important, not only in Rioja but in other regions, too. Look out for terms such as *crianza* and *reserva* to indicate barrel maturation.

• Sparkling wines and Champagnes have a language of their own. *Brut* means 'dry' the world over. It is important to look out for this word on a label if you want to avoid sugary froth. The term *méthode traditionnelle* is worth spotting, too, as it indicates the best method of making fizz, now adopted in various regions which make quality bubbly (see pages 114–119).

• Somewhere on all bottles there will be the following information: the alcohol level (which can vary a great deal), the volume of liquid in the bottle (usually 75cl), the country of origin and the producer. It's likely that some phrase will indicate oak-ageing, if this took place, and the back label may tell you more about the region, the blend of grapes and the winemaker's aims. Other back labels will simply give you a load of hot air about the romantic peaks of the Chilean Andes or the sun-soaked vineyards of the warm Barossa Valley!

TIPS FOR BUYING WINE

Even those with a good knowledge of wine can find it pretty disarming to be faced with rows of bottles in a supermarket or off-licence. It's clearly easier to grab a familiar bottle every time, but as I have made clear throughout this book, that can mean you get stuck in a boring rut, always drinking the same grapes from the same region and even the same producer. The world of wine is so richly endowed with different styles that it would be a shame to get fed up with the liquid in your glass.

So the first and most essential tip to the wine shopper is be prepared to experiment. Make a point of avoiding a bottle that is tried and tested in your house; instead plump for something quite different, be it a new grape variety – how about Viognier, Sémillon, Cabernet Franc? Or a new region: Greece, Uruguay and Portugal are all fascinating right now. In particular, avoid the very big brands. There may be nothing wrong with them, and they may well represent reasonable quality, reliable wine at a decent price, but *everyone* drinks them and they usually fail to offer much excitement. With smaller producers you are more likely to get a handcrafted, characterful product. And besides, your neighbours won't all have it in their wine racks too.

Think about the various outlets that offer wine and decide which ones work best for you on different occasions. Supermarket wine departments have been thoroughly revolutionised since the late twentieth century and these outlets stock an impressive range of styles and price points. Their turnover is fast, so wines are likely to be fresh, and they can offer worthwhile discounts because of their buying power. Supermarkets are convenient, of course, as you can buy your booze at the same time as your weekly food shop and choose wines that match your cooking easily.

On the other hand, some argue that supermarkets still lack the knowledgeable assistance offered by a specialist merchant. A fine wine merchant is certainly a great place to go if you are searching for something different and might need some help in choosing. Make sure you quiz the assistant hard and perhaps even ask for a taste of wine – independents sometimes have a bottle or two of interesting stuff open to try.

It's worth seeking out a specialist merchant if you are developing a love of a particular type of wine. And there are now a few impressive smaller outlets with a serious emphasis on non-European wines. Don't forget mail order or internet

wine buying, too. Make sure that you always use a well-established, reputable company, however.

Look out for 'bin end' offers, which indicates the end of a stock of wine (a few bottles left over that are being sold at a special price). In general, though, be sure to avoid wines that are past it, looking tired and stewing gently on a dusty shelf.

Finally, take a good look at any information you are offered in-store: shelf descriptions or press recommendations (not a fool-proof guide to your own likes and dislikes, but probably a fair indication of the style of wine), labels, leaflets and in-store magazines. We all need as much help as possible when buying wine if we can't actually taste the stuff, so make good use of what is there to help you decide. Above all else, trust your own tastebuds and get sampling as much as possible.